COLLEGE OF AL

At ✳ Issue

Does the Internet Benefit Society?

Cindy Mur, *Book Editor*

Bruce Glassman, *Vice President*
Bonnie Szumski, *Publisher*
Helen Cothran, *Managing Editor*

GREENHAVEN PRESS
An imprint of Thomson Gale, a part of The Thomson Corporation

THOMSON
—— ✳ ——™
GALE

Detroit • New York • San Francisco • San Diego • New Haven, Conn.
Waterville, Maine • London • Munich

THOMSON

———————★———————™

GALE

LIBRARY OF CONGRESS CATALOGING-IN-PUBLICATION DATA

Does the Internet benefit society? / Cindy Mur, book editor.
    p. cm. — (At issue)
Includes bibliographical references and index.
ISBN 0-7377-2706-3 (pbk. : alk. paper) — ISBN 0-7377-2705-5 (lib. : alk. paper)
    1. Internet—Moral and ethical aspects. 2. Internet—Social aspects.
3. Computer network resources. I. Mur, Cindy. II. At issue (San Diego, Calif.)
TK5105.878.D64 2005
303.48'33—dc22   2004062800

Printed in the United States of America

Contents

Introduction

Few would disagree that the Internet has become an important part of the daily life in American society. Its use is often taken for granted by the estimated 50 million Americans now online. Many Americans use the Internet to stay in touch with friends and family or to make new friends through chat rooms. While the Internet provides unlimited opportunities for meeting others, these opportunities can be both useful and dangerous.

One of the more direct ways that the Internet facilitates social meetings is through online dating services. Online dating makes it easy for busy or isolated people to meet others with similar interests. According to Jupiter Research, in 2003 more than 17 million people viewed online personal ads and more than 2 million paid for a personal ad. Moreover, many people have met and married through online dating services. Match.com estimates that more than two hundred thousand members found the person they were seeking through its service. Once regarded as the last hope for desperate singles, personal ads are now considered an efficient way to meet potential romantic partners.

For conversation and companionship without romance, the Internet provides opportunities for people to discuss hobbies and shared interests. Fantasy football, stamp collecting, books, and politics are only a few topics one can chat about online. In fact, the sole function of some Web sites is to provide a forum for discussion. One such site, Meetup.com, boasts that over a million people have joined its "Meetup Groups" worldwide. This site hosts groups to discuss more than four thousand topics, ranging from chess to Elvis to gardening.

The politically minded have opportunities to discuss politics in Internet chat rooms. Many sites provide a forum for people to debate and even to organize to protest a government action or to show support for a candidate or cause. During the 2004 U.S. presidential primaries, for example, groups of people would meet up in chat rooms to discuss Howard Dean's candidacy. The meeting times were planned on Meetup.com. Both the popularity of "meetups" and support for Dean's candidacy grew, as reported by Andrew Boyd in the *Nation*. He writes,

4

"Nationally, the 500 people who had signed up for Dean meetups in January [2003] grew to 60,000 by mid-July." Another Web site, United for Peace and Justice, was the launching point for the worldwide demonstrations in early 2003 against the war in Iraq, as people met and planned protest rallies on this site.

The Internet also provides help for those seeking support or comfort: For those grieving the loss of a loved one, for instance, Legacy.com offers guest books where grief-stricken families may read condolences left by friends or family members from far away. These guest books also serve as meeting places where bereaved visitors connect and share their tragedies.

The Internet serves as a place of connection for survivors of adversity as well. A study published in the *British Medical Journal* in March 2004 examines the way cancer patients use the Internet. The study found that these patients used the Internet not only to research information about their condition but also to "seek support and experiential information from other patients." The study also notes that patients would be unlikely to find this level of information and support through conventional means.

Although the Internet offers a variety of useful ways for people to connect with others throughout the world, it can also be dangerous or just unpleasant because some people use it as a tool for deception. For example, some users lie about their background, marital status, and physical condition on Internet dating sites. According to journalist David Batstone, "Online daters report that the people they meet often do not resemble their online photos, nor does their online persona always match real-life character." In fact, the once meteoric growth in online dating has begun to flatten out, with many people choosing not to renew their membership. One such member of Match.com found that "more than a few of the handsome, rugged, athletic types she thought she had been corresponding with looked more like George Costanza than George Clooney. Some of those 'single' guys turned out to have wives," according to an article in the *San Diego Union-Tribune* newspaper.

Although lying to a dating service is dishonest, the action usually causes emotional distress rather than bodily injury. Unfortunately, the Internet can also be used by the unscrupulous to prey upon the unsuspecting in violent ways. Pedophiles lie in wait in children's or teens' chat rooms, sometimes luring them to meet in person. Once a child has taken the bait, he or she is often kidnapped, abused, or raped. Paul J. Becker, professor of criminology at Morehead State University in Morehead, Kentucky, outlines a few examples:

In February 2001 a man was arrested for kidnapping and sexual assault after he used the Internet to lure a 15-year-old Florida girl to Greece. . . . A 2000 article in *The Columbus Dispatch* recounted online crimes in Ohio, including one in which a junior high school teacher used his computer to engage in "pillow talk" with several students, and another in which a man flew to Houston to have sex with a 13-year-old boy he met online.

Police units nationwide that investigate Internet crime describe a multitude of these stories in which young children and teens are lured into dangerous situations by pedophiles.

Pedophiles and sexual predators are not the only threats on the Internet. Racists and hate groups also use Web sites and discussion groups to spread their message of hate to young people. In 2001 there were an estimated twenty-eight hundred hate group Web sites encouraging violence and hatred toward people of color, Jewish Americans, and gays. Some sites offer games for children to play along with rhetoric supporting "white pride," attempting to normalize racism for kids.

Another group of dangerous sites is those that encourage the development of mental illnesses such as anorexia, bulimia, and self-mutilation. These sites offer tips to young women and teens for successfully starving or hurting themselves and provide positive reinforcement for such behavior. These sites also contain chat rooms or message boards on which these unhealthy users learn further ways to hurt themselves.

Many praise the Internet as a tool that offers nearly unlimited information at the click of a mouse. However, given the dangers of the Internet described above, users need to exercise caution and self-control. The authors in *At Issue: Does the Internet Benefit Society?* present a variety of viewpoints on the many beneficial uses of the Internet, the controversy over its threats, and the effect it has on society.

1

The Internet: An Overview

Charles Dubow

Charles Dubow is an executive editor at Forbes.com, *an on-line financial magazine.*

The U.S. Defense Department created the Internet in 1969 to facilitate communication between military bases and universities. Initially, the Internet was difficult to use, and early personal computers were not able to access it. However, the introduction of system protocols—standards that allowed computers to talk to each other—in 1989 made the Internet available to anyone with a telephone line. As individual users accessed the new World Wide Web to send e-mail, "talk" in chat rooms, or purchase products, companies began to see the Web's profit potential, and began creating their own Web pages and buying advertising space on Web sites. In the future, every television will be connected to the Internet and information will be accessed more quickly with an increased rate of data transmission, called bandwidth.

When I initially went online, I hated it. The year was 1994, and I had decided to finally use one of those CD-ROMs that kept arriving in the mail, uninvited, from AOL [an online service provider]. All right, I thought, I'll give it a shot and see what this Internet thing is all about. So I unplugged my fax, plugged the phone line into my computer, inserted the disk and heard for the very first time that distinctively annoying high-pitched whistle that informs AOL users they are about to enter cyberspace. Then, alas, I was told that no connection could be

Charles Dubow, "Untangling the Web," *Town & Country*, vol. 154, June 2000. Copyright © 2000 by The Hearst Corporation. Reproduced by permission of the author.

made and to try again later. I did—about three years later.

Still, I was intrigued by this new form of communication. In 1994 there were rumblings that the Internet was more than just a place for computer-science geeks and conspiracy theorists; that the "Information Superhighway," as it was being called, would one day replace newspapers, television, all media as we knew it. It was already apparent that the Internet was a huge financial engine—Microsoft's Bill Gates, Oracle's Larry Ellison, Intel's Andy Grove and many others were well on their way to amassing vast fortunes. It was clearly something to learn more about.

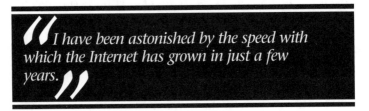

I have been astonished by the speed with which the Internet has grown in just a few years.

I got my chance in 1997 when I was hired as an editor at Forbes' new online magazine, *Forbes.com.* I had no Internet experience, but that didn't seem to matter, since almost none of my colleagues did either. I felt like the biggest fraud in the group, however, because I had no technical bona fides whatsoever. Math had always been my least favorite subject in school. Video games bored me, as did almost all types of consumer electronics. I didn't care whether Apple or Microsoft had the superior operating system because I didn't know there was a difference—or, for that matter, what an operating system even was. I was firmly an analog man in an increasingly digital World. And I had no desire to change.

But I have changed, and so too has the Internet. Like millions of others, I have been astonished by the speed with which the Internet has grown in just a few years. This growth has been partly fueled by the extraordinary success of Internet-related shares on the stock market, but it is also the result of technological improvements that have made the Internet so much easier—and less expensive—to use. Today [2000] almost half of all adults in the U.S. have access to the Internet, either at home or at the office. Grandmothers can view pictures of their grandchildren online; consumers can purchase everything from toys and clothing to furniture and airline tickets. Stocks can be traded, weather updates checked, doctors consulted.

But what exactly is the Internet? Is it a vast repository of information? A cyber shopping mall? A forum in which complete strangers can spend hours chatting with each other? A new form of entertainment? A way to make both local and long-distance calls? An engine for economic growth? In fact, it is all these things, and the beauty of it is that each year it becomes capable of so much more. . . .

The Rise of the Internet

The Internet has been around since 1969. It was known then as the ARPANET (Advanced Research Projects Agency Network) and was created by the Department of Defense to allow information to flow between geographically separated computers, largely at military bases and universities, over a private network. When a number of large corporations, such as IBM, were asked if they wanted access, they scoffed at the idea and proclaimed that it would never work.

True, it was a roughly formed thing and it wasn't very user-friendly—full of digital codes and number sequences that were unintelligible to most people. But it was highly effective. Written communication could flow instantly across the country at the stroke of a key, so that by 1972 scientists were using the network as much for sending electronic messages (e-mail) as for sharing data. Two years later, the term "Internet" was coined.

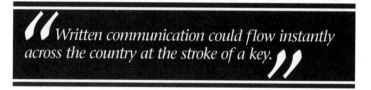

Written communication could flow instantly across the country at the stroke of a key.

But the Internet was the electronic equivalent of a secret handshake, thanks in large part to the high cost and limited capabilities of computers. This was before [computer companies] Dell and Apple, PCs [personal computers] and laptops were part of the popular lexicon. The computers that were in existence were enormous air-cooled, room-size machines—whales with brains the size of a pea.

That all changed in the mid-seventies, when such companies as Commodore (now defunct) and Texas Instruments began offering small personal computers—basically, typewriters with the features of a calculator—costing a few hundred dollars. Suddenly, computing was in the hands—comparatively speaking—of the masses.

But the Internet still wasn't. These early personal computers could no sooner access the Internet than a Smith-Corona [typewriter] could. It would take more than a smaller computer to get people online; the tiny brains that tell computers what to do—known as microchips—had to become smaller too. The trick was to shrink them further without making them less powerful and to make them in sufficient numbers to keep costs low. Companies such as Intel set about solving this problem through silicon technology (and since most of the companies were located down the peninsula from San Francisco, the name "Silicon Valley" took root). Today the speed and brainpower of an Intel Pentium III chip, currently available in many PCs, is equivalent to that of a supercomputer from a decade ago.

Creating the Web

Internet usage would evolve more slowly. Sure, it required smaller, faster, cheaper computers, but it also needed two other vitally important things: a language that would allow all the information available on the Internet to be packaged and disseminated in an easy-to-read manner, and a way to connect individual computers to the Internet.

In 1989, Englishman Tim Berners-Lee, a researcher at the Organisation Europeenne pour la Recherche Nucleaire (CERN) in Geneva, proposed the idea of the World Wide Web, an international system of "protocols." Essentially common grammatical tools of a technological language, protocols allow for conversations between any two computers so that anyone anywhere can search for and receive (or, conversely, create and send) text, graphic images, and audio and video files.

The problem of getting everyone online, however, was trickier and is still being addressed. Currently most people access the World Wide Web via a telephone line plugged into a modem (modulator-demodulator) that is either built into or attached externally to a computer. But the telephone networks weren't designed to handle the kind of data that the Internet pushes over their lines, and the connection speeds are often maddeningly slow. While the telephone companies have for years offered special dedicated lines (T-1s and T-3s) to those willing to pay thousands of dollars per month, until recently most people had to be content with the snail's pace of a dial-up connection.

Going online became known as the World Wide Wait.

All the same, by the mid-1990s millions of people were going online, from either their homes or offices. E-mail was one of the most popular attractions, as was a new form of interaction called "e-chat." Exploding across the Internet were chat rooms in which complete strangers could correspond electronically about topics ranging from dithyrambs to dating (although usually a lot more of the latter).

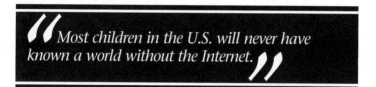

Most children in the U.S. will never have known a world without the Internet.

Large corporations too were slowly waking up to the potential benefits of connecting their employees to the Internet. Even more exciting, entrepreneurs began to see the opportunities in creating new businesses exclusively for the Net. In the 1990s such pioneers as America Online, Sun Microsystems, Inktomi, Yahoo! and Cisco caught the attention of Wall Street with their eye-popping initial public offerings and sky-high valuations. To give an idea of the kind of money we're talking about, $10,000 invested in each of these stocks at their IPOs [initial public offerings] would, as of March [2000], have been worth $2.4 million collectively. AOL alone had seen its stock rise 50,000 percent before it announced its intention to buy Time Warner in January.

The Growth of the Web

By 1996 the Internet was growing steadily, though it was still the preserve of a small percentage of the U.S. population, with only 15.2 million households online out of a total of about 103 million. But in just four years that number has more than tripled, to 51.5 million, and by 2005 it is expected that as many as seventy-five million households will be online (with, increasingly, more people accessing the Internet using mobile devices such as digital cell phones, pagers and Palm Pilots).

The majority of the "early adopters" using the World Wide Web were, for the most part, young, affluent and educated. It didn't take long for merchants to realize that all these people made an attractive potential market. In the mid-1990s a number of online vendors began experimenting with e-commerce; i.e., selling goods and services over the Internet. Initially, the kinds of products that were available were small, easy-to-ship items such as books, CDs, toys and the like. Amazon.com, which got its start as an online bookseller, was among the first to successfully stake out territory on the Internet. Now everything from a Boeing jet to an ink-jet printer is available on the Web. The Internet research firm IDC goes so far as to predict that the amount of commerce conducted over the World Wide Web will top $1.6 trillion by 2003.[1]

There is also big money at stake as both major advertisers and tradition-minded Madison Avenue [New York advertising] agencies (who decide whether to place their clients' ads in print venues, television or radio) begin to realize that the Internet is more than hype. The key to realizing the Web's economic potential as an advertising medium at this point seems to lie in creating advertising that is more compelling than the current crop of horizontal "banners" that run at the top or bottom of Web pages or the square "buttons" strategically placed within these pages' main texts. The new generation of ads will incorporate full-motion video, so they look like TV commercials—but with the extra dimension of interactivity (advertisers want consumers to be able to buy their products directly from their computers).

The Internet of the Future

In fact, as the technology improves, computers will become more like televisions (a phenomenon now popularly known as "convergence"), if not actually replace them. Already a few companies are designing—and in some places offering—a primitive form of interactive TV, the best-known version of which is Microsoft's WebTV. The new set-top boxes that the cable TV and telecommunications companies are offering are digital—which means they can receive more bandwidth, hence more channels, than is possible through the existing cable—and have the capability to be interactive. Interactivity is more than watching a pizza ad and then instantly ordering a pizza. It also will allow you to send and receive e-mail, surf the Net, hold long-distance teleconferences and view practically any

1. Total Internet sales in 2004 were estimated to be $69.2 billion, according to the Census Bureau of the Department of Commerce in Washington, D.C.

movie ever made. You'll even be able to watch, say, the U.S. Open and simultaneously find out who the women's champions were over the past ten years and buy tickets to next year's tournament, all with the click of a button.

Within a few years nearly every new TV in the U.S. may be capable of being connected to the Internet, and at that point the distinction between computers and televisions will truly start to vanish. Those computers that are left will be used purely for advanced processing tasks or word processing, but most homes will have at least one set-top box through which every form of data flows. This box will be in the den, the bedroom, the office, even the kitchen—wherever it makes the most sense for your lifestyle. It will probably also connect to such smart appliances as refrigerators, with microprocessors and embedded screens that not only will let people know when they've run out of eggs—and order a new dozen—but will allow them to search the Internet for the perfect frittata recipe.

To get to that point, Americans will need to connect to the Internet faster, which will require more bandwidth. That can happen only when the cable television, telecommunications and satellite companies are able to upgrade their networks to carry broadband. Last year [1999] such companies as AT&T, MCI WorldCom and Bell Atlantic spent billions on the acquisition of satellite access and the upgrade of existing cable. . . . It is not enough, though, to deploy broadband: the Cable, telecommunications and satellite companies must make their broadband offerings cheap enough to appeal to the mass market.

Already prices are coming down, and by 2005 more than twenty-eight million homes and businesses are expected to have a broadband connection through either cable, DSL or wireless technology. At that point, most children in the U.S. will never have known a world without the Internet; by then it will have become so easy to use that even the most technophobic adult will be able to surf with ease. More and more people will be able to telecommute, conducting live business meetings from their living rooms. And on their lunch hour, they'll be able to tour a museum, order groceries or even pay their taxes.

But the world won't change completely. Just as television didn't kill off the movies, some things will never translate to the Web. The perfect fresh peach can't be tasted electronically. Couture will still have to be bought in Paris. A walk on the beach can't be enjoyed online. And, on a rainy afternoon, nothing will beat curling up on the couch with a well-loved book.

2

The Internet Has a Positive Effect on Education

Kathleen Medina et al.

Kathleen Medina is associate director of the California History–Social Science Project at the University of California– Los Angeles. Matthew Pigg taught seventh grade at Holmes Junior High School in Davis, California, and is currently director of technology for the University of California's Teacher Education and Professional Development department. Gail Desler teaches fifth and sixth grades at Morse Elementary School in Sacramento, California. Gil Gorospe teaches seventh and eighth grades at Eich Intermediate School in Roseville, California.

The Internet has brought about a revolution in teaching that reformists have been trying to achieve since 1986. Teachers are no longer the focal point in the classroom, but instead facilitate their students' learning. The Internet ends classroom isolation, allowing the development of relationships between teachers and parents and students, and between students and the rest of the world. The Internet also allows quiet or shy students to have a voice in the classroom because they can use tools such as e-mail to communicate with teachers. It creates learning environments that help students respond to and connect with their world. The Internet also facilitates classroom cooperation.

A t least since the Carnegie Commission's 1986 report, *A Nation Prepared* [which called for sweeping changes in education], education reformers and policy makers have been campaigning for a changing role for teachers—but for reasons other than the impact of technology and computer use. Teachers have been encouraged to become a "guide on the side" rather than the traditional "sage on the stage." Shortly thereafter, in 1988, [educational researchers] Kathleen Devaney and Gary Sykes described a new "conception of teaching that emphasizes the continual and changing interplay between thought and action, based on close observation and reflection about the encounter or 'match' between students and subject matter," so that teaching would be "more than skilled transmission" but would become "principled action."

In one fell swoop, the technology revolution may accomplish what 10 years of education reform could not. The preparation that we have traditionally provided for teachers no longer allows them to maintain the status of "sage" with any credibility. They cannot know as much as the Internet can make available to their students.

The good news is that there are a few teachers in cyberspace. Like their media-savvy students, they know that computer technology can vanquish the problems that have plagued schools for a century: the problems of parochialism and isolation; the problems of lack of time, space, and support for teacher communication; the problem of articulating with teachers and students across grade levels; the lack of easy access to subject-matter experts and to lively and up-to-date resource materials; and even the challenge of providing a wider audience for student work and student writing. The "force" is with these teachers, and, just as in the George Lucas film [*Star Wars*], the force is a belief in a sense of community and interconnectedness that can be facilitated by technology. The revelation for us has been that computers are about relationships. Below, we offer three cyberspace stories from the experience of three of the authors.

Matt's Story

I grew up with computers. While the other kids were spending the summers lacing wallets, riding ponies, and coming home with cases of poison oak, I was at computer camp. When I was in the fourth grade, I played [the computer game] Oregon Trail over a 200-baud modem with a connection to a VAX [line of computers] mainframe. Oh, the reams of paper we wasted! I programmed, word-processed, and spread-sheeted my way through high school and college. So naturally, when I began teaching in 1991, I wanted to integrate the use of computers into my classroom.

The marriage of computer technology with my teaching, however, was rocky from the start. I kept telling myself, "Teaching and technology are perfect for each other, and they will just have to work through a few incompatibilities to become a match made in heaven." I did not realize until recently that my focus on technology was missing the point.

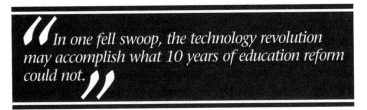

In one fell swoop, the technology revolution may accomplish what 10 years of education reform could not.

My mantra, a typical one, had been that "computers are tools and should be used to increase student productivity and efficiency." Thus, while I experimented with the Internet and a few software programs, in the classroom I focused primarily on word processing to encourage writing fluency and to minimize the drudgery of rewriting and editing. And while the computer did prove to be a motivator for reluctant writers and certainly increased the effort most students gave to rewriting, I gradually realized that this use of computers hardly represented a significant change from traditional schooling.

The advent of Internet access in the classroom, however, is truly beginning to change the face of schooling. When I first stepped into the classroom 10 years ago, I was not prepared for the profound sense of isolation I would feel. While this isolation allows teachers great freedom in their classrooms, it can also become professionally stifling. When teachers close the doors to their classrooms, the entire world—including colleagues and parents—is shut outside. It is a rare classroom that actually has even a telephone to help bridge the barrier between school and the rest of the world.

When schools wire their classrooms for the Internet, it is not the "access to information" that changes the classroom. There is already too much information. What changes the classroom—for teachers, students, parents, and the community—is the end of the isolation. Now that I have access to the Internet in my classroom (still no phone, mind you), I have a way to connect almost instantly with nearly every parent of my 150 students, and I can contact an individual parent or the entire group.

This may seem trivial to those outside education, but trying to maintain contact with 15 different parents while planning an end-of-the-year field trip is next to impossible to do well over the telephone—especially when the closest phone sits on someone else's desk, 200 yards from my classroom. Maintaining contact via an e-mail list becomes a breeze—not only for me, but for those 15 busy parents who need to keep abreast of who will be bringing pizzas and where students need to be picked up. These e-mail contacts have had a dramatic impact on my ability to communicate effectively with parents.

The impact of our communication has been profound and somewhat unexpected. After I began using e-mail almost exclusively for planning events some four years ago, the resulting evolution of communication and community was fascinating to watch. What began as an e-mail list of parents working together to plan a field trip developed into an ongoing community of parents discussing issues as wide-ranging as reading lists for the summer and a search for parents willing to run for school board. The parents quickly became a powerful resource that my students and I could tap for their expertise, experience, and knowledge. As Alan November [a leader in education technology] says, "It's not about information or the technology; it's about relationships."

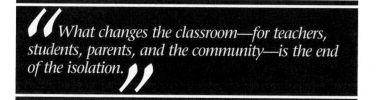

What changes the classroom—for teachers, students, parents, and the community—is the end of the isolation.

While dramatically improving the relationships with parents and the community has been one result of Internet access, the relationships students are able to develop with learning and with their world are even more exciting. Three years ago, while doing some research on an Arab country, one of my students met a citizen of Morocco in a chat room. Not only was my student able to ask the Moroccan questions about her country, but she also made a human connection with someone who had a very different social, political, and religious view of the world. Their interaction and the excitement it produced in my student made me recognize that I needed to reorganize dramatically the way I taught so that interactions and relationships were central to my teaching rather than the result of a chance encounter by a motivated student. As part of an online collaborative venture with teachers throughout California, I have rewritten the Arab unit to make human connection an integral part of the learning. Now, as we study Islam, students will take part in an online discussion group and be able to ask practicing Muslims from other countries about their religion. In this way, students make connections that are far richer than any textbook or library could offer.

The Internet will change classrooms in many ways, but the most dramatic and important changes that I have seen are those that end the artificial isolation. The traditional model of schools is so deeply ingrained that it is not easy for most of us to imagine the myriad ways schools can be reformed by using the Internet to build relationships between teachers and parents, parents and parents, teachers and teachers, students and teachers, and students and the rest of the world. I do not deny the beauty of the Internet as a research tool, but if we are searching for major changes in education, they will come only when we bring local and global communities into the schoolroom.

Gail's Story

The Internet is changing both my approach to teaching history and my students' approach to learning. Today, when I sit down to prepare a unit of study, I am more likely to be in front of my computer than at the library. Within seconds of contacting my "virtual librarian" (a search engine), I can locate a rich array of grade-appropriate lessons and resources. Compared to my pre-Internet days, I am able to produce research-based lessons more quickly. As for my students, as I watch them tap into regional and global sites from a phone line limited to local calls only, I can see that their learning is no longer confined by the walls of the classroom. They too are locating worlds of online resources and learning. My fifth- and sixth-graders have already joined "generation.com."

The Internet is more than lessons and resources, though. Middle school students often struggle to find a voice in the classroom. With 34 students to a class and a packed curriculum, it is not always possible for me to provide for small-group and one-on-one discussions. And the reality of whole-class discussions is that many student voices, especially those of the shy or less confident, go unheard. My students have found a comfortable solution that allows them to voice their thoughts at any time: e-mail. For the past year, a growing number of students who would rarely—perhaps never—willingly raise their hands and speak out in class are now e-mailing me regularly. They are indeed finding a voice in the classroom—a powerful electronic one.

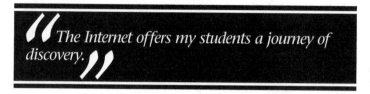

The Internet offers my students a journey of discovery.

The Internet offers my students a journey of discovery and allows them to pose a multitude of questions related to the past and to sort out the answers in terms of present and future issues. A common discovery, we are finding, is that history does not happen in a vacuum; it happens in our own communities. Last year, for instance, my fifth-graders read *Journey to Topaz*, a novel about the internment of Japanese Americans. One group of students opted to create an online museum for their book report. Using a wealth of Internet sources, they paired scenes from the novel with online primary sources such as documents and photographs. Several students conducted e-mail interviews with actual "children of the camps," and a local educator who spent her early years in the internment camp at Jerome very willingly provided them with a firsthand account of how Executive Order 9066[1] changed her life and that of everyone else in Elk Grove, California—our community. The end product was a student-designed Web page that has taken them far beyond the novel.

1. After Japan bombed Pearl Harbor on December 7, 1941, the United States entered World War II, and many Americans developed a great deal of hatred and resentment toward Japanese Americans—fueled by fear. As a result, on February 19, 1942, President Roosevelt signed Executive Order 9066, which allowed military commanders to designate areas "from which any or all persons may be excluded." Under this order, most Japanese and Americans of Japanese ancestry were removed from western coastal regions and interred in camps until the war was over.

My classroom reflects California's changing demographics and its increasing cultural pluralism. Yet too often I have watched students look into their history books and see where they are not. I want my students to know that there is more than one chapter in our nation's immigration story. I want them to know the importance of Angel Island—the western port of entry for immigrants. I want them to challenge the notion of Ellis Island [a port of entry in New York] as the sole symbol of immigration. The personal immigration stories of many of my students began when their parents, grandparents, or great-grandparents crossed the Pacific, not the Atlantic, to start new lives in the United States.

Over the summer I met a teacher from the Dalton School in New York City. She too wanted her students to know about the other chapters in our immigration story. Last week, we each took our classes on a field trip. While her class explored Ellis Island, mine explored Angel Island. We have linked our Web pages and posted student-generated questions for each class to research. The end product will be a virtual field trip to both ports of entry. While it is unlikely that the students in our classrooms will ever meet one another in the flesh, over the course of the school year they can form an active community of learners.

Each time I venture with my class across the electronic frontier, I see the difference that access to information and online relationships can make for students, beginning with their enthusiasm and ending with the final product. I agree with Matt: it's not about technology. It's about creating classrooms that reflect, respond to, and connect with a changing world.

Gil's Story

"I got an e-mail from Sweden!" "So did I!" Soon a whole chorus of students excitedly proclaimed that they had heard from their "keypals" in Sweden. The connection with Sweden—and a similar one with Japan—was part of a unit of study on the various ethnic groups that have come to the U.S. Like Gail, I had found that immigration was a subject readily adaptable to Internet research. My students had brainstormed questions to ask their keypals about school life, teen life, and cultural life in Sweden. The students then used the Internet to download historical pictures and stories about the immigrant experience, which served as the basis for a hypothetical immigrant's scrapbook.

Last year marked a time of exploration and experimentation for me on ways to use computers to teach my eighth-graders. It began when my district offered me the opportunity to train social studies teachers at my school in the use of technology. I took the job because I was curious about how technology might enhance my teaching, and I was glad for the opportunity to explore that with my colleagues. The director of the district's technology program encouraged me to apply for a grant to win Pentium II computers, and I won seven. When the school upgraded its computers, I inherited the old ones, which brought my total to 26. It was the opportunity I had dreamed of: my own computer lab, so that I could experiment.

> **//** *The Internet is a tool that gives my students the independence they seek in order to pursue what they want to learn.* **//**

As a teacher of history, I have become used to doing my own research to create source-based lessons. I decided that I would not invest a lot of money in CD-ROM programs because they are expensive, inflexible, and quickly become out-of-date. I wanted the Internet to be the primary tool my students would use for their research.

On our first visit to the computer lab for a geography unit, my students planned a vacation around the U.S. and created a map of the places they would visit. The Internet gave them the information they needed to locate businesses, parks, and historical and geographical landmarks. In the process, I observed that the students wasted a lot of time searching, so I knew I needed to create my own website "filter" to guide them in their research. I took a class on how to do that and discovered that it was quite easy. . . .

Internet research made it possible for my students to engage in one of the most exciting events of the year: the California History Day competition. The theme for 1998–99 was how an invention had affected history, and it was made to order for Information Age computer devotees.

During the research for the competition, I learned a lot more about how to guide my students to use the Internet. I needed to teach them to recognize valid sources of information, to fine-tune their searching, and to document and cite their findings for the bibliography. For example, we covered how to tell the differences between government, education, museum, or corporate sites; how to identify perspective and judge credibility; and how to select and incorporate sources from a variety of viewpoints. Of course, they also taught me. One team of students who were researching the impact of fiber optics in society asked permission to e-mail current experts on the Internet to get more information.

Three teams of five students each from our school won first place in our county competition. When we went to Disneyland for the state competition, two of the teams were finalists.

Now, after a few days in the classroom, I invariably hear, "Are we going to the lab today?" When the students and I are in the computer lab, my role as teacher becomes one of facilitator. The Internet is a tool that gives my students the independence they seek in order to pursue what they want to learn. Because many of their assignments and research projects demand cooperative learning, I oversee the groups' work. As I move from group to group, the scene comes alive and transforms into something akin to the CBS newsroom facing a deadline. I overhear the probing questions, I see students excitedly sharing discoveries, and I watch many of them rush to assist classmates who are less proficient in using the technology. Learning becomes tangible, and the walls—between us and the past, between us and the world, and between us and one another—come tumbling down.

3

Internet Commercialism Harms Education

Bettina Fabos

Bettina Fabos is an associate professor in the Department of Communication Studies at the University of Northern Iowa in Cedar Falls, Iowa.

Since 1995, when school Internet use began to mushroom, teachers have increasingly found that advertising on the Internet interferes with their students' research and education. As they research, students must constantly navigate around distracting pop-up and banner ads. Unfortunately, capitalism has turned the Web into a "commercial highway" that, like television, film, and radio before it, has succumbed to powerful corporate interests that undermine its integrity. Users are increasingly being directed to commercial sites while valuable public and nonprofit sites are being marginalized.

W hen I began this [writing], all the students, media specialists, and teachers I talked to had great respect for the worldwide web as an educational medium. Perhaps the most passionate advocate of all was one English teacher, Steve Le-Rouge. Great in the classroom and passionate about the web, he was more familiar with online resources than most people. He had his students use the web for numerous class projects and even taught a special unit in webpage critique. In fact, he was so optimistic about the web in education that he made me feel as if online commercialism—the focus of my study—was no big deal. "Teachers don't have to be that savvy," he told me. "Kids

Bettina Fabos, *Wrong Turn on the Information Superhighway: Education and the Commercialization of the Internet.* New York: Teachers College Press, 2004. Copyright © 2004 by Teachers College, Columbia University. All rights reserved. Reproduced by permission of the publisher.

know a spiel when they see one. They've been exposed to spiels all their lives. Kids do know about commercialism and they don't get taken in easily." Steve was far more worried about government efforts to filter "adult" web content from school sites than he was about internet commercialization.

But 3 years later my research was done, and I emailed some of my conclusions to Steve. As usual, he was smart and funny, but he also had a different mindset from the pure optimism he showed before. Steve was clearly getting fed up with the onslaught of commercial messages that were obstructing his students' research and learning. Indeed, his reply to me amounted to a scathing indictment of what the web had become:

> The pop-up ads alone are annoying, but many (probably most) sites also sandwich whatever article is of interest between columns of advertisements. Even pretty reputable sites like Time.com or ScientificAmerican.com throw pop-ups and columns of ads at the students; even .org sites like pbs.org want to sell you stuff at their "Shop PBS" link! For the most part, if the research topic is a traditional social issue topic like date rape or alternative fuels or sports injuries, the students can pretty much ignore the ads. But, when the research topic is a little more "edgy," the ads follow suit, and then I know I have trouble:

> "Hey, Chris, c'mon over here and check out this cool bong!"

> "No way, man, that's just not possible!"

> "Fer real! They're usin' .50 caliber casings for the bowl!"

> "Aw, that's just too whack!"

> You get the idea. Do anything on designer drugs or music censorship or legalization of drugs or street racing and I spend 90 percent of my time puttin' out fires. I even had a "good" student (who, I know, wouldn't intentionally stray) get locked into a porn loop when he followed a link on F1 racing. Go figure. I had a student do a paper on disc golf this last semester. Since there are no traditional sources on the topic, his paper was almost

entirely based on Internet sources. Do you have any idea how many ads there are for sports equipment and diet supplements on sports-related sites? Once he was past the blizzard of pop-ups and flashing ads, he still had to navigate the homepages, which are designed to give you no real information, but only links, which trigger another wave of pop-ups and ads. Sometimes the actual articles are three or four layers deep. Oy Vey!

Steve was now grappling with online commercialism, which has grown from annoying online ads to something much larger. And that's what this . . . is about. It's about what capitalism has done to the web, turning what was promised as an "information highway" into a commercial highway in every classroom. Not only has advertising become more pervasive, but commercial interests have also undermined the integrity of search engines and compromised the educational value of most of the web's vast holdings. . . .

Schools Become Connected

The year 1995 was a pivotal one in the history of communication technology. It was the year the internet took off in schools —the most exciting communication technology in education since television, 30 years earlier. Educators, librarians, parents, and internet promoters called the new medium a library of information at children's fingertips, and identified the internet as a panacea for education. It was the year President [Bill] Clinton first "challenged" all American classrooms to get onto the information superhighway, citing research that the internet would drastically help at-risk students. It was the year community members across the United States gave up their weekends to roll up their sleeves, pull cables, and wire schools. These "netdays" were heavily publicized in local papers and on local TV. Even President Clinton and Vice President [Al] Gore (who had coined the term *information superhighway*) donned their work clothes to participate in several NetDay wiring efforts.

The year 1995 was also when several high-profile advertising campaigns began promoting the internet as a key to greater knowledge and as a technology for both an educational and democratic revolution. The blitz of print and television advertisements portrayed children poised in front of their computers, enthralled with the "knowledge" pouring directly into their brains. Some ads touted that children gave up recess time to stay inside and interact online. In other ads, children magically floated above their desks, buoyed by their imagination and the online conversations they were having with real astronauts. The ads *en force* suggested that children, with their proficient keying skills and easy grasp of technology, were savvy drivers on the information highway, more adept, even, than adults.

The year 1995 was also the year that Microsoft leader Bill Gates published his bestseller *The Road Ahead*, which introduced his vision of the "Connected Learning Community" via the internet. Gates publicized the book with speeches all over the United States, expounding on the educational promise of internet technology and donating the proceeds of his book to support technology in public schools. It was the year when the internet was surely positioned as an educational technology.

Today, the information highway looks more like a shopping mall than a library.

Most significantly, amid the extensive campaign to exult prospects of the internet for public education, 1995 was the year that the internet became privatized. Built over the previous 3 decades with government-supported, publicly funded programs, the internet's U.S. backbone was quietly sold to telecommunications and computer giants in 1995. Thus, at the same time that the prominent rhetoric about education and knowledge was in ascendance, powerful corporate interests were reshaping the internet as a commercial tool. And its ubiquity was growing. By 2000, more than 97% of U.S. schools had internet access; a majority of U.S. homes and offices were connected as well. In 5 short years, the internet had become a mass medium, achieving this benchmark more quickly than any communication technology before.

The Commercialization of the Internet

To any student of media history, the commercialization of the internet should come as no surprise. Every major communication technology, despite its initial promise as a medium for greater education and democracy, has been overtaken by commercial interests. Film, which promoters claimed would replace textbooks and make all learning visual, did not last long as an educational technology: Its high cost of production resulted in dreadful educational film content. The slickest educational film productions were often just thinly veiled corporate public relations pieces for the classroom. Film would serve the entertainment industry, not education.

Radio, which was more affordable and accessible than film, had greater promise as an educational medium. Initially developed, like the internet, by grassroots efforts and government investment, radio found teachers and students as its earliest adopters. Radio's early success in education, however, was soon squashed by the intense power and lobbying efforts of the commercial radio industry. U.S. public airwaves were won by commercial interests in 1934, although unlike with the internet, there was intense debate over the matter. Then came television, which was hobbled as an educational tool because it was based on radio's commercial model from its inception. Furthermore, the high cost of broadcast TV production made it an uneconomical educational tool. All these technologies would not serve education, no matter how promising. The internet, it now seems, is following suit.

Today, the information highway looks more like a shopping mall than a library. By 1999, researchers had already determined that 83% of the web served commercial purposes, with only 6% serving science/education (defined as serving university, college, and research interests). Commercial advertisements, most commonly in the forms of interactive banner, pop-up, and pop-under displays, dominate the web. But more consequentially, commercial services have successfully managed to route users from *all* that the worldwide web has to offer into an increasingly finite and incestuous web of commercial enterprise.

Narrowing Internet Choices

First, commercial web-navigation services, which initially generated income through web display ads, now make much more revenue by directing users to the websites of clients who pay for such placement. Content directories such as LookSmart and America Online (AOL) and commercial search engine providers such as Overture accept payments for prominently displaying commercial websites within their directories or search-result lists. Overture's strategies, which are now common practice in the search engine industry, illustrate the extent to which commercial online ventures are willing to sacrifice content and neutrality for profit. Even the one search engine provider that uses rigorous methods to maintain integrity in searches—Google—still ends up with search results that are inevitably skewed by the enormity of commercial sites now dominating the web.

Then there are the intensifying efforts among the largest media companies to funnel web content (and web users) into increasingly narrow channels, which are either owned by them or are in partnership with them. With their dominance as internet service providers (ISPs) and email and instant messaging service providers, and with their strong brand-name identification, companies such as Time Warner, Yahoo!, and Microsoft can more easily control the way people use the web and the breadth of information people can locate online. This is not to say that there are not incredible, valuable, and wonderful websites that offer a host of different ideas and a wealth of information. . . . The internet does indeed belong in the classroom. No technology since radio has so captivated educators' attention. The medium has enormous potential as a place to share ideas, as a place to publish school projects, and as a place for educators to join together and exchange teaching methods and lesson plans. It has enormous potential as a research tool, as a library, and as a laboratory. As a vehicle for written, audio, and visual communication, the internet has unprecedented flexibility and adaptability.

Indeed, citizens and schools already use the internet for education and many are using it well. But the end result of the internet's now extensive commercialization is that users continue to be directed to an abundance of commercial sites—some valuable, many not—while other potentially valuable online materials are being marginalized as public and nonprofit online spaces are becoming increasingly difficult to find. This is both a problem for educators, who have no organized response to these developments, and all citizens, for the success of the internet as a democratic medium and educational tool is dependent upon a plurality of voices.

4

The Internet Aids Hate Groups

Les Back

Les Back is the head of the Centre for Urban and Community Research at Goldsmiths College in London.

A growing number of white supremacist groups are using the Internet to spread their message of hate. Stormfront, the first racist Web site, provides chat rooms to promote the discussion of the ideology of white power and to recruit new members to racist groups. The Aryan Dating Page offers a personal ad service for white supremacists. Although the growth of racist activism on the Internet is disturbing, many Net racists do not have a strong long-term commitment to white power politics and are unlikely to create a global racist movement. However, there is a real danger that a white supremacist could use information available on the Internet, such as recipes for bombs, to commit acts of racist terrorism.

After celebrating the Internet as a digital nirvana in which democracy and free speech flourish, we are finally uncovering the dark side in which racists and xenophobes not only broadcast their propaganda in cyberspace but also ply their paraphernalia and hate through international networks. However, the spate of scare stories about the burgeoning tide of racist online materials ignores the ultimate question: is the face of racism changing?

Most articles focus exclusively on the number of websites, virtual discussion groups and chat rooms spreading the messages of white supremacist groups like the Ku Klux Klan, White

Les Back, "White Fortresses in Cyberspace," *UNESCO Courier*, January 2001. Copyright © 2001 by the United Nations Educational, Scientific, and Cultural Organization. Reproduced by permission.

Aryan Resistance and the British National Party, which first seized the Internet as an unregulated and relatively cheap media in the mid-1990s. While there is no doubt that these sites and groups are growing, accurate estimates are difficult to calculate. To investigate hate on the Net, you must combine the skills of a detective, a lie detector and propaganda code breaker. For online materials are part of a digital masquerade that conceals as much as it shows. You cannot simply count and record web addresses because of the frequency in which pages are posted and taken down. However, experts agree that there are hundreds of sites, perhaps as many as 3,000.

Much of the debate about hate on the Net has revolved around censorship. Internet Service Providers (ISP) may voluntarily prohibit use of their servers and install filters along with web browsers to prevent access to key racist sites. But it is almost impossible to regulate the Net as a whole. The debate about censorship has become a cul-de-sac because of the seemingly irreconcilable tension between the libertarian ethos of free speech and the difficulty in defining the limit of what is morally acceptable to say or write. To some extent, the polemic overshadows the critical issue: what is drawing people into the racist Net world?

"WHITE PRIDE WORLDWIDE"—with this slogan, Don Black of the U.S. launched the world's first and most notorious racist website, Stormfront, on March 27, 1995. Black, a former Klansman, learned his computer skills in a federal prison in Texas where he compulsively worked on the prison's Radio Shack TRS-80 computer at U.S. taxpayers' expense. Once out of jail, Black put his new skills to work to build an international system of followers by offering a trans-local notion of race.

Racists Are Connecting in Cyberspace

Consider this passage from an e-mail sent to Stormfront: "I am a 20-year-old white American with roots in North America dating back 300 years and then into Europe, Normandy, France. Well anyways, I am proud to here [hear] of an organization for the advancement of whites."

Racists like Black are basically using the Internet to foster a notion of whiteness that unites old world racial nationalisms (i.e. in Europe and Scandinavia) with the white diasporas of the New World (i.e. United States, Canada, South Africa, Australia and New Zealand and parts of South America). Despite the diversity of racist groups in cyberspace, they share a common language of race and white solidarity. Firstly, this notion of whiteness promotes a racial lineage that is plotted through, and to a large extent sustained in cyberspace. The Internet is the technology of globalization, interconnecting permeable human cultures. Yet in the racist Net-world, the Internet is used to foster an ethos of racial separation. With the goal of establishing "white fortresses" in cyberspace, these racists are forging new connections between ultra right-wing sites in North America, Western Europe and Scandinavia at a considerable pace. Yet, it is still the American websites and news groups that are the most sophisticated and the most active.

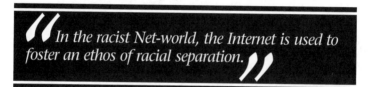

In the racist Net-world, the Internet is used to foster an ethos of racial separation.

The big question remains exactly how many people are being drawn into racist activism by the Net? Recently, Alex Curtis—self-proclaimed "Lone Wolf of hate" from San Diego and producer of the extremist magazine *The Nationalist Observer*—claimed to "reach 100s–1000s of the most radical racists in the world each week." However, it is dangerous to over-estimate the level of activity. The number of white racists regularly involved in the Internet globally is somewhere between 5,000 and 10,000, divided into 10 to 20 clusters. Once again, it is impossible to offer anything other than an educated guess. The number of "hits" on a web page, for example, need not indicate "sympathetic inquiries," rather they could include opponents, monitoring agencies and researchers. The key point is that these relatively small numbers of people can have a significant presence.

White Supremacists Use Online Personal Ads

Not only are they using the Net for recruitment, but attempts are also being made to combine cyber-activism with that of the "real world." For example, the RaceLink web page offers a list of activists' contact details and locations around the world. Additionally, The Aryan Dating Page (now posted on Stormfront) offers a contact service for white supremacists. While most of the profiles are American, there are also personal ads from a range of countries including Brazil, Canada, Holland, Norway, Portugal, U.K., Slovakia and Australia as well as from white South Africans.

> **// The number of white racists regularly involved in the Internet globally is somewhere between 5,000 and 10,000, divided into 10 to 20 clusters. //**

One of the interesting things about scrolling through the personal ads is that the faces that appear are nothing like the archetypal image of "The Racist." There are very few skinheads with Nazi tattoos: these white supremacist "lonely hearts," mostly in their twenties and thirties, look surprisingly prosaic. Take 36-year-old Cathy, who lives in the U.S. state of Pennsylvania, which is far from an ethnic melting pot, but who is "desperate to move to a WHITE area!" She appears in the photograph in a rhinestone outfit with glitzy earrings: "The picture of me is a little overdone," she explained. "I had photos done with the girls at the office . . . I look like an Aryan Princess when I get dressed up. But I am really the girl-next-door type." Or, 19-year-old Debbie from New England, who wrote: "I am [a] young white power woman who seeks someone seriously devoted to the white power movement. A person whose commitment is undaunting. I would like to speak with men who share the same values as I."

The male ads provide an equally unexpected set of portraits of white supremacy. Frank, a 48-year-old divorced single parent from Palo Alto, California, writes: "Today I'm a responsible parent and have my views but don't go out of my way to let it be known unless confronted. I have tattoos, and am down for the Aryan race. So hope to hear from you fine ladies in the near future." Here Frank presents himself as a kind of white supremacist "new man." This is contrasted with John Botti's ad, a 25-year-old from Los Altos who presents himself as a preppy, "going places" kind-of-guy. He wrote: "I am looking for some who is as conservative and pretty as hell. Equally as important is someone with a quality education." These are images of fascism in the information age that bear little resemblance to previous incarnations. This was brought home very powerfully by the image of Max, a 36-year-old Canadian, who described himself as a "long-time Movement activist." He listed his interests as anthropology, Monty Python's humour, the *Titanic* story, Celtic music and [U.S.] Civil War re-enacting. Max chose to have his photograph taken at his computer keyboard, where he presents himself as the picture of technological proficiency. This struck me, the first time I saw it, as a very appropriate image of the face of today's racism.

Power Struggles in the Racist Movement

However, these postmodern portraits of racism are coloured by fragmented and multiple identities little suited to the disciplined organization of "real world" racist politics. In this mercurial world, can the ideology and commitment to racism be turned off as quickly as the computer? There is some evidence to suggest that Net racists have a rather chaotic affiliation to white power politics. For example, American Milton J. Kleim, who was once the self-styled "Net Nazi Number 1," renounced his politics almost overnight.

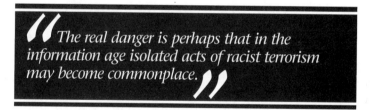

The real danger is perhaps that in the information age isolated acts of racist terrorism may become commonplace.

Kleim first became involved through Usenet, a network of online news groups, as a student in 1993. But he didn't have a face-to-face meeting with anyone in the racist movement until he graduated in 1995. Less than a year later, he abandoned racism altogether. In an e-mail interview he commented: "The act of leaving was painful, and the aftermath stressful [. . .] I essentially became a 'nonperson,' and I haven't really been denounced [. . .] I only received two or three harassing phone calls from displeased movement adherents. . . . The saddest part is that my 'movement' experience was my most exciting, most rewarding time in my life," he commented. "I've moved from National Socialism to Misanthropy." Racist culture offered Kleim a sense of purpose through an online identity and a temporary resolution to existential crisis. This same sense of purpose comes through in many interviews with Net racists. What is equally true is that this does not last and the virtual mask of racial extremism can be quickly cast off.

Not only does individual commitment appear shaky, but so do the larger networks of Net-based racist groups. In the "real world," each group generally revolves around or owes its existence to a charismatic leader who takes on the initiative of forging alliances. These agreements, however, are generally short-lived because of power struggles between the various leaders. In cyberspace, this fall-out seems to be occurring at an even faster pace. Basically, the condensed rate of exchange in cyberspace shortens the fuse for an explosion. The vituperative online feud between Harold A. Covington of the National Socialist White People's Party, William L. Pierce of the National Alliance and both sets of their supporters (in the U.S.) is perhaps the best example of this syndrome. Reflecting on "The Future of the White Internet," Covington wrote:

> The Net is being viciously and tragically abused by a shockingly large number of either bogus or deranged "White Racists" [. . .] I think it is too early just yet to quantify just how the lunacy interacts with, counteracts and affects the impact of the serious political work. It is like panning for gold in a flowing sewer; both the raw and toxic sewage and the gold are there, and the question is how much gold any individual can extract before the fumes and the corruption drive him off—or until he keels over and falls in and becomes part of the sewer system.

The racist use of the Internet is not about to deliver a mass global racist movement. In this sense, the imitators of fascism and Nazism are not in the same league as the zealots of yesteryear. Yet the significance of this phenomenon should not be sought in the numbers of activists.The fact that those involved remain relatively small should not be read as a comforting statistic. What, then, is the nature of this threat? The real danger is perhaps that in the information age isolated acts of racist terrorism may become commonplace. In this respect the 1999 London bombing campaign conducted by David Copeland—who found his "recipe" for nail bombs on the Net—may be an indication of the form that racist violence will take in this millennium. These acts are perpetrated by individuals whose prime contact with racist politics is via their computer keyboards.

5

The Internet Facilitates Crime

Terrence Berg

Terrence Berg is an assistant U.S. attorney in Detroit assigned to the economic crimes unit. Previously, he ran the High-Tech Crime Unit in the Michigan attorney general's office.

The Internet provides criminals with abundant opportunities for wrongdoing. For example, offenders can steal personal information, commit fraud (such as taking money but not delivering merchandise), solicit child pornography, or launch damaging computer viruses. Criminals are able to communicate with each other easily on the Internet and share ideas, reinforcing their antisocial beliefs. Also, the Internet provides millions of prospective victims for criminals who can operate anonymously. As a result, law enforcers must now work harder and need greater training and better equipment to capture Internet criminals.

L ooking over the shoulder of the police detective at his computer monitor, I felt my stomach churn. He was posing as a 14-year-old girl in a chat room. Within moments, a strange man, age 42, was making a proposition. With so many positive media reports focused on the miracles of the Internet as a communication and education tool, the convenience and profits of e-commerce and the spectacular but now fading boom in dot-com stocks, little attention has been paid to the dark side of the Internet and its impact on society's ability to fight crime. Unfortunately, although the Internet is unquestionably a marvelous tool for good, the widespread use of computers and the Internet has created new challenges for law enforcement while simultaneously offering advantages to criminals.

Computers and the Internet are commonly being used in criminal activities in three ways. First, computers are repositories of stored digital evidence. From home computers to laptops to wireless cell phones and Web-enabled Palm Pilots, computers are rich in electronic records: e-mail communications, financial records, telephone numbers, logs of Web-surfing activity—the very same kind of information one might find in an old-fashioned filing cabinet. Second, computers are used by criminals as tools to commit traditional crimes, as in Internet fraud (online auction failure-to-deliver fraud is skyrocketing), child solicitation and child pornography distribution, sale of contraband, threats and harassment. Third, computers, and sometimes entire networks, are made the targets of criminal conduct. Examples include hacking, theft of information, virus launching and denial of service attacks.

The Internet Criminal's Advantage

A central advantage the Internet offers to those disposed to sociopathic behaviors is that it creates the possibility for the first time for such individuals to find one another, to congregate in online communities, to share ideas and to provide one another with the potent benefit of group reinforcement for their antisocial attitudes.

The Internet has made it possible for predators to find entire online fraternities of pedophiles with which to share experiences.

Take the example of child sexual predators. Such offenders always existed in the real world and victimized children when they found the opportunity. Because pedophilia is shunned and criminalized by organized society, however, child predators felt the strong constraints of social norms preventing them from acting out their criminal intentions, and they would rarely risk the attempt to find like-minded cohorts. The Internet has made it possible for predators to find entire online fraternities of pedophiles with which to share experiences, to transmit child pornography instantly and anonymously to one another and experience the comfort of a reassuring support group. Worse yet, modern encryption technology also makes it possible for all these transmissions to be hidden in virtually unbreakable code.

Just as the pedophile can now find his 'niche' on the Net, so can the credit card fraudster, the frustrated neo-Nazi or the suicide-minded teenager.

Unfortunately, the example of the child predator is only one of many. Because the Internet is as broad as the human psyche, it naturally encompasses all of the darkest manifestations of evil imaginable: every form of denigration of human dignity and antisocial behavior, from racial hatred and white supremacist ideology, to self-mutilation, torture and sadomasochism, to virulent misogynism, to violent extremism and Satanism. Web sites and chat rooms dedicated to glorifying such behaviors—as well as more mundane unlawful conduct such as hacking, credit card fraud, tax evasion and the manufacture of illegal drugs and explosives—are easily located by entering simple search terms into any Internet search engine. And once inside such sites, one finds more and more of them by clicking on hyperlinks within them, in a seemingly endless downward spiral. Just as the pedophile can now find his "niche" on the Net, so can the credit card fraudster, the frustrated neo-Nazi or the suicide-minded teenager, as we saw so tragically in the case of the Columbine high school killings.

It is impossible to assess the impact that the availability of new "cyber-support groups for antisocial behavior" will have on the ability of society to respond to crime. But there is no question that this new reality is a "net positive" for the bad guys that did not exist prior to the advent of the Internet.

Two other strategic advantages the Internet offers criminals are its almost limitless pool of victims and its veil of anonymity. Fraud artists seeking to victimize investors or persuade consumers to send money in advance for nonexistent goods can reach a vast number of possible victims cheaply and effectively through the Internet without ever risking any personal contact or identification. Not only can criminals use the Internet to prey on a worldwide community, they can also do so with comparatively greater anonymity than they have in the real world. This is true because it is possible for a criminal to use false information when registering his Web site or his free e-mail account, to forge e-mail headers to obscure his identity, to use "anonymizer" services that purposely hide a user's identifying information, or for a hacker to connect through numerous systems—including some in foreign countries—before eventually launching his attack on a victim.

The Police at a Disadvantage

In addition to granting these advantages to criminals, the Internet also raises the bar for law enforcement, making investigations harder than they were before there was cyberspace. Internet crime, though local in its impact on victims, is national and even worldwide in its scope. Thanks to the networked world, for example, it is more and more likely that electronically stored records—such as e-mail files that are being sought by authorities in connection with an investigation—will be physically stored outside the local jurisdiction on an e-mail server half a continent away. This means that local prosecutors may need to serve subpoenas on service providers throughout the nation. The legal enforceability of such investigative subpoenas is not entirely clear, and may require seeking the assistance of authorities in another state. Similarly, if search warrants from one state need to be executed in another jurisdiction, it may mean that investigators must either travel to the other state and participate in the search, or depend on their sister law enforcement agencies for assistance. The latter likewise might extend to requiring the other jurisdiction's officers to travel to the prosecuting state to provide testimony.

These cases are harder and more costly to investigate. If an Internet scam artist is caught in his home jurisdiction, it is likely that there may be only a few victims located in that same state, though there may be hundreds of others scattered across the country. To establish the full scope of the crime, officials of the county where the defendant is located may need to spend money to transport numerous out-of-state witnesses to testify so that the whole story can be revealed. The high cost of handling prosecutions with victims in multiple jurisdictions is another strategic disadvantage faced by law enforcement in the networked world.

The main practical challenge this new kind of criminal activity creates is the need for training for both investigators and prosecutors so that they will be able to handle these new high-tech cases. Catching cybercriminals requires well trained and better equipped cybercops, and this is an expensive proposition, but it is one that the Internet revolution has laid at society's doorstep. Dealing with this practical need, the delivery of training and equipment to law enforcement officers and prosecutors, will require a continuing commitment by society. Whether such a commitment will be made, however, remains to be seen. Perhaps policymakers and the public will be more willing to allocate such resources when they consider some of the negative strategic consequences that the criminal usage of the Internet presents.

Because the general public's use of this technology is barely 10 years old, the full extent of the Internet's impact on society's ability to cope with crime is still a matter of speculation. Certainly the Internet's phenomenal benefits to society in terms of information availability, convenient e-commerce and increased communication must be factored positively into any assessment. But as things stand at the start of the 21st century, law enforcement has some serious catching up to do, and policymakers will need to commit significant resources in order to ensure that there is a sheriff on the electronic frontier.

6

The Threat of Cyberterrorism Is Greatly Exaggerated

Joshua Green

Joshua Green is editor of the Washington Monthly *news-magazine.*

Since the terrorist attacks of September 11, 2001, the federal government and the media have made numerous statements about the threat of terrorists using computers to launch a catastrophic attack on the United States. However, the dangers of cyberterrorism are in fact minimal. No one has ever been able to kill someone using a computer. Furthermore, computers that control nuclear weapons and airliners have extremely strong security systems. Although terrorists could hack into some systems that control infrastructure, such as electric power grids and gas utilities, these systems could be quickly repaired. The hysteria over cyberterrorism is fueled by private agendas. Technology companies eager to sell their security products benefit from the fervor over cyberterrorism. The government in turn exaggerates the threat in order to generate more public anxiety about terrorism and thus garner more support for its war on terror.

A gain and again since [the terrorist attacks of] September 11, President [George W.] Bush, Vice President [Dick] Cheney, and senior administration officials have alerted the public not only to the dangers of chemical, biological, and nuclear weapons but also to the further menace of cyberterrorism. "Terrorists can sit at one computer connected to one network and can create worldwide havoc," warned Homeland Security Director Tom Ridge in a representative observation [in April 2002]. "[They] don't necessarily need a bomb or explosives to cripple a sector of the economy, or shut down a power grid."

Even before September 11, Bush was fervently depicting an America imminently in danger of an attack by cyberterrorists, warning during his presidential campaign that "American forces are overused and underfunded precisely when they are confronted by a host of new threats and challenges—the spread of weapons of mass destruction, the rise of cyberterrorism, the proliferation of missile technology." In other words, the country is confronted not just by the specter of terrorism, but by a menacing new breed of it that is technologically advanced, little understood, and difficult to defend against. Since September 11, these concerns have only multiplied. A survey of 725 cities conducted by the National League of Cities for the anniversary of the attacks shows that cyberterrorism ranks with biological and chemical weapons atop officials' lists of fears.

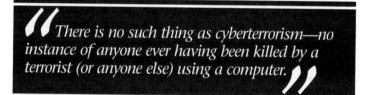

There is no such thing as cyberterrorism—no instance of anyone ever having been killed by a terrorist (or anyone else) using a computer.

Concern over cyberterrorism is particularly acute in Washington. As is often the case with a new threat, an entire industry has arisen to grapple with its ramifications—think tanks have launched new projects and issued white papers, experts have testified to its dangers before Congress, private companies have hastily deployed security consultants and software designed to protect public and private targets, and the media have trumpeted the threat with such front-page headlines as this one, in *The Washington Post* [in June 2002]: "Cyber-Attacks by Al Qaeda Feared, Terrorists at Threshold of Using Internet as Tool of Bloodshed, Experts Say."

The federal government has requested $4.5 billion for infrastructure security next year [2003]; the FBI boasts more than 1,000 "cyber investigators." President Bush and Vice President Cheney keep the issue before the public; and in response to September 11, Bush created the office of "cybersecurity czar" in the

White House, naming to this position Richard Clarke, who has done more than anyone to raise awareness, including warning that "if an attack comes today with information warfare . . . it would be much, much worse than Pearl Harbor."

A Major American Fear

It's no surprise, then, that cyberterrorism now ranks alongside other weapons of mass destruction in the public consciousness. Americans have had a latent fear of catastrophic computer attack ever since a teenage Matthew Broderick hacked into the Pentagon's nuclear weapons system and nearly launched World War III in the 1983 movie *War Games*. Judging by official alarums and newspaper headlines, such scenarios are all the more likely in today's wired world.

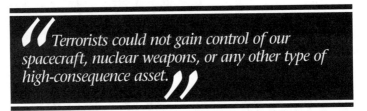

Terrorists could not gain control of our spacecraft, nuclear weapons, or any other type of high-consequence asset.

There's just one problem: There is no such thing as cyberterrorism—no instance of anyone ever having been killed by a terrorist (or anyone else) using a computer. Nor is there compelling evidence that al Qaeda or any other terrorist organization has resorted to computers for any sort of serious destructive activity. What's more, outside of a Tom Clancy novel, computer security specialists believe it is virtually impossible to use the Internet to inflict death on a large scale, and many scoff at the notion that terrorists would bother trying. "I don't lie awake at night worrying about cyberattacks ruining my life," says Dorothy Denning, a computer science professor at Georgetown University and one of the country's foremost cybersecurity experts. "Not only does [cyberterrorism] not rank alongside chemical, biological, or nuclear weapons, but it is not anywhere near as serious as other potential physical threats like car bombs or suicide bombers."

Which is not to say that cybersecurity isn't a serious problem—it's just not one that involves terrorists. Interviews with terrorism and computer security experts, and current and former government and military officials, yielded near unanimous agreement that the real danger is from the criminals and other hackers who did $15 billion in damage to the global economy [in 2001] using viruses, worms, and other readily available tools. That figure is sure to balloon if more isn't done to protect vulnerable computer systems, the vast majority of which are in the private sector. Yet when it comes to imposing the tough measures on business necessary to protect against the real cyberthreats, the Bush administration has balked.

Hollywood Scenarios

When ordinary people imagine cyberterrorism, they tend to think along Hollywood plot lines, doomsday scenarios in which terrorists hijack nuclear weapons, airliners, or military computers from halfway around the world. Given the colorful history of federal boon-doggles—billion-dollar weapons systems that misfire, $600 toilet seats—that's an understandable concern. But, with few exceptions, it's not one that applies to preparedness for a cyberattack. "The government is miles ahead of the private sector when it comes to cybersecurity," says Michael Cheek, director of intelligence for iDefense, a Virginia-based computer security company with government and private-sector clients. "Particularly the most sensitive military systems."

Serious effort and plain good fortune have combined to bring this about. Take nuclear weapons. The biggest fallacy about their vulnerability, promoted in action thrillers like *War Games*, is that they're designed for remote operation. "[The movie] is premised on the assumption that there's a modem bank hanging on the side of the computer that controls the missiles," says Martin Libicki, a defense analyst at the RAND Corporation. "I assure you, there isn't." Rather, nuclear weapons and other sensitive military systems enjoy the most basic form of Internet security: they're "air-gapped," meaning that they're not physically connected to the Internet and are therefore inaccessible to outside hackers. (Nuclear weapons also contain "permissive action links," mechanisms to prevent weapons from being armed without inputting codes carried by the president.) A retired military official was somewhat indignant at the mere suggestion: "As a general principle, we've been looking at this thing for 20 years. What cave have you been living in if you haven't considered this [threat]?"

When it comes to cyberthreats, the Defense Department has been particularly vigilant to protect key systems by isolating them from the Net and even from the Pentagon's internal network. All new software must be submitted to the National Security Agency for security testing. "Terrorists could not gain control of our spacecraft, nuclear weapons, or any other type of high-consequence asset," says Air Force Chief Information Officer John Gilligan. . . . [Since late 2001], Pentagon CIO [chief information officer] John Stenbit has enforced a moratorium on new wireless networks, which are often easy to hack into, as well as common wireless devices such as PDAs [personal digital assistants], BlackBerrys, and even wireless or infrared copiers and faxes.

Unjustified Concerns

The September 11 hijackings led to an outcry that airliners are particularly susceptible to cyberterrorism. [In 2002], for instance, Sen. Charles Schumer (D-N.Y.) described "the absolute havoc and devastation that would result if cyberterrorists suddenly shut down our air traffic control system, with thousands of planes in mid-flight." In fact, cybersecurity experts give some of their highest marks to the FAA [Federal Aviation Administration] which reasonably separates its administrative and air traffic control systems and strictly air-gaps the latter. And there's a reason the 9/11 hijackers used box-cutters instead of keyboards: It's impossible to hijack a plane remotely, which eliminates the possibility of a high-tech 9/11 scenario in which planes are used as weapons.

Another source of concern is terrorist infiltration of our intelligence agencies. But here, too, the risk is slim. The CIA's classified computers are also air-gapped, as is the FBI's entire computer system. "They've been paranoid about this forever," says Libicki, adding that paranoia is a sound governing principle when it comes to cybersecurity. Such concerns are manifesting themselves in broader policy terms as well. One notable characteristic of [2001's] Quadrennial Defense Review was how strongly it focused on protecting information systems.

But certain tics in the way government agencies procure technology have also—entirely by accident—helped to keep them largely free of hackers. For years, agencies eschewed off-the-shelf products and insisted instead on developing proprietary systems, unique to their branch of government—a particularly savvy form of bureaucratic self-preservation. When, say, the Department of Agriculture succeeded in convincing

Congress that it needed a specially designed system, both the agency and the contractor benefited. The software company was assured the agency's long-term business, which became dependent on its product; in turn, bureaucrats developed an expertise with the software that made them difficult to replace. This, of course, fostered colossal inefficiencies—agencies often couldn't communicate with each other, minor companies developed fiefdoms in certain agencies, and if a purveyor went bankrupt, the agency was left with no one to manage its technology. But it did provide a peculiar sort of protection: Outside a select few, no one understood these specific systems well enough to violate them. So in a sense, the famous inability of agencies like the FBI and INS [Immigration and Naturalization Service] to share information because of incompatible computer systems has yielded the inadvertent benefit of shielding them from attack.

What About Infrastructure?

That leaves the less-protected secondary targets—power grids, oil pipelines, dams, and water systems that don't present opportunities as nightmarish as do nuclear weapons, but nonetheless seem capable, under the wrong hands, of causing their own mass destruction. Because most of these systems are in the private sector and are not yet regarded as national security loopholes, they tend to be less secure than government and military systems. In addition, companies increasingly use the Internet to manage such processes as oil-pipeline flow and water levels in dams by means of "supervisory control and data acquisition" systems, or SCADA, which confers remote access. Most experts see possible vulnerability here, and though terrorists have never attempted to exploit it, media accounts often sensationalize the likelihood that they will.

To illustrate the supposed ease with which our enemies could subvert a dam, *The Washington Post*'s June [2002] story on al Qaeda cyberterrorism related an anecdote about a 12-year-old who hacked into the SCADA system at Arizona's Theodore Roosevelt Dam in 1998, and was, the article intimated, within mere keystrokes of unleashing millions of gallons of water upon helpless downstream communities. But a subsequent investigation by the tech-news site CNet.com revealed the tale to be largely apocryphal—the incident occurred in 1994, the hacker was 27, and, most importantly, investigators concluded that he couldn't have gained control of the dam and that no lives or property were ever at risk.

Most hackers break in simply for sport. To the extent that these hacks occur, they're mainly Web site defacements, which are a nuisance, but leave the intruder no closer to exploiting the system in any deadly way. Security experts dismiss such hackers as "ankle biters" and roll their eyes at prognostications of doom.

Of course, it's conceivable that a computer-literate terrorist truly intent on wreaking havoc could hack into computers at a dam or power company. But once inside, it would be far more difficult for him to cause significant damage than most people realize. "It's not the difficulty of doing it," says RAND's Libicki. "It's the difficulty of doing it and having any real consequence." "No one explains precisely the how, whys, and wherefores of these apocalyptic scenarios," says George Smith, the editor of *Crypt Newsletter*, which covers computer security issues. "You always just get the assumption that chemical plants can be made to explode, that the water supply can be polluted—things that are even hard to do physically are suddenly assumed to be elementary because of the prominence of the Internet."

> **//***Numerous technology companies . . . have recast themselves as innovators crucial to national security and boosted their Washington presence in an effort to attract federal dollars.***//**

Few besides a company's own employees possess the specific technical know-how required to run a specialized SCADA system. The most commonly cited example of SCADA exploitation bears this out. . . . [In 2000], an Australian man used an Internet connection to release a million gallons of raw sewage along Queensland's Sunshine Coast after being turned down for a government job. When police arrested him, they discovered that he'd worked for the company that designed the sewage treatment plant's control software. This is true of most serious cybersecurity breaches—they tend to come from insiders. It was Robert Hanssen's familiarity with the FBI's computer system that allowed him to exploit it despite its security. In both cases, the perpetrators weren't terrorists but rogue employees with specialized knowledge difficult, if not impossible, for outsiders to acquire—a security concern, but not one attributable to cyberterrorism.

Damage Would Be Limited

Terrorists might, in theory, try to recruit insiders. But even if they succeeded, the degree of damage they could cause would still be limited. Most worst-case scenarios (particularly those put forth by government) presuppose that no human beings are keeping watch to intervene if something goes wrong. But especially in the case of electrical power grids, oil and gas utilities, and communications companies, this is simply untrue. Such systems get hit all the time by hurricanes, floods, or tornadoes, and company employees are well rehearsed in handling the fallout. This is equally true when the trouble stems from human action. . . . [In 2000] in California, energy companies like Enron and El Paso Corp. conspired to cause power shortages that led to brownouts and blackouts—the same effects cyberterrorists would wreak. As Smith points out, "There were no newspaper reports of people dying as a result of the blackouts. No one lost their mind." The state suffered only minor (if demoralizing) inconvenience.

But perhaps the best indicator of what is realistic came [in 2002] when the U.S. Naval War College contracted with a research group to simulate a massive attack on the nation's information infrastructure. Government hackers and security analysts gathered in Newport, R.I., for a war game dubbed "Digital Pearl Harbor." The result? The hackers failed to crash the Internet, though they did cause serious sporadic damage. But, according to a CNet.com report, officials concluded that terrorists hoping to stage such an attack "would require a syndicate with significant resources, including $200 million, country-level intelligence and five years of preparation time.". . .

Exploiting Fears of Cyberterrorism

Yet Washington hypes cyberterrorism incessantly. "Cyberterrorism and cyberattacks are sexy right now. It's novel, original, it captures people's imagination," says Georgetown's Denning. Indeed, a peculiar sort of one-upmanship has developed when describing the severity of the threat. The most popular term, "electronic Pearl Harbor," was coined in 1991 by an alarmist tech writer named Winn Schwartau to hype a novel. For a while, in the mid-1990s, "electronic Chernobyl" was in vogue.

[In 2002], Sen. Charles Schumer (D-N.Y.) warned of a looming "digital Armageddon." And the Center for Strategic and International Studies, a Washington think tank, has christened its own term, "digital Waterloo."

> *The danger of hyping a threat like cyberterrorism is that once the exaggeration becomes clear, the public will grow cynical toward warnings about real threats.*

Why all this brooding over so relatively minor a threat? Ignorance is one reason. Cyberterrorism merges two spheres—terrorism and technology—that most lawmakers and senior administration officials don't fully understand and therefore tend to fear, making them likelier to accede to any measure, if only out of self-preservation. Just as tellingly, many are eager to exploit this ignorance. Numerous technology companies, still reeling from the collapse of the tech bubble, have recast themselves as innovators crucial to national security and boosted their Washington presence in an effort to attract federal dollars. As Ohio State University law professor Peter Swire explained to *Mother Jones*, "Many companies that rode the dot-com boom need to find big new sources of income. One is direct sales to the federal government; another is federal mandates. If we have a big federal push for new security spending, that could prop up the sagging market."

But lately, a third motive has merged: Stoking fears of cyberterrorism helps maintain the level of public anxiety about terrorism generally, which in turn makes it easier for the administration to pass its agenda. . . .

Political Motivations

The danger of hyping a threat like cyberterrorism is that once the exaggeration becomes clear, the public will grow cynical toward warnings about real threats. The Chicken Little approach might be excusable were the Bush administration hyping cyberterrorism in order to build political momentum for dealing with the true problem posed by hackers and shoddy software. . . .

There were high hopes, then, for the Bush administration's

National Strategy to Secure Cyberspace—the culmination of a year's effort to address the country's post-9/11 cybersecurity problems. [Presidential adviser Richard] Clarke's team circulated early drafts that contained what most experts considered to be solid measures for shoring up security in government, business, and home computers. But the business community got word that the plan contained tough (read: potentially costly) prescriptions, and petitioned the White House, which gutted them. When a draft of the plan was rolled out in mid-September [2002], Bill Conner, president of the computer security firm Entrust, told *The Washington Post*, "It looks as though a Ph.D. wrote the government items, but it reads like someone a year out of grade school wrote the rest of the plan."

It's hard to imagine a worse outcome for all involved, even private industry. By knuckling under to the business community's anti-regulatory impulses, Bush produced a weak plan that ultimately leaves the problem of cybersecurity to persist. It proposes no regulations, no legislation . . . , prompting most security experts to dismiss it out of hand. What it does do instead is continue the stream of officially sanctioned scaremongering about cyberattack, much to the delight of software companies. IT [information technology] security remains one of the few bright spots in the depressed tech market and thus that important sector of the market is perfectly satisfied with the status quo. But as the Nimda virus proved, even companies that pay for security software (and oppose government standards) don't realize just how poorly it protects them. So in effect, the Bush administration has created the conditions for what amounts to war profiteering—frightening businesses into investing in security, but refusing to force the changes necessary to make software safe and effective.

The way the Bush White House has exaggerated the likelihood of cyberterrorism is familiar to anyone who's followed its style of government. This is an administration that will frequently proclaim a threat (the Saddam/al Qaeda connection, for instance) in order to forward its broader agenda, only to move on nonchalantly when evidence proves elusive or nonexistent. But in this case, by moving on, Bush leaves unaddressed something that really is a problem—just not one that suits the administration's interests. Forced to choose between increasing security and pleasing his business base, the president has chosen the latter. Hyping a threat that doesn't exist while shrinking from one that does is no way to protect the country.

7

The Internet Improves Medical Care

George C. Halvorson and George J. Isham

George C. Halvorson is chairman and chief executive officer of Kaiser Foundation Health Plan, Inc., and Kaiser Foundation Hospitals, in Oakland, California. George J. Isham is a physician who works with HealthPartners, a group of non-profit Minnesota health care organizations. He is also a member of the board of directors of the Minnesota Health Data Institute.

More people are accessing the Internet for health information. As a result, they are better informed but are also more demanding as patients. Patients may suggest care options to their doctors based on information they have read on the Internet, resulting in improved treatment. Doctors also benefit from using the Internet because they can access information about treatment more easily than ever before. In the near future, e-visits with physicians will cut down on patient emergency room visits and may make specialty consultations over long distances a reality. Although some misleading or bad information is present on the Internet, overall patient care has improved because of patient and doctor use of the Web.

The Internet has become a major cost factor in health care. Because of the Internet, patients are better informed, more demanding, and have higher expectations for their care. The volumes of Internet use are immense: almost 100 million adult Americans now [in 2003] use the Internet for health care in-

George C. Halvorson and George J. Isham, *Epidemic of Care: A Call for Safer, Better, and More Accountable Health Care.* San Francisco: Jossey-Bass, 2003. Copyright © 2003 by George C. Halvorson and George J. Isham. All rights reserved. Reproduced by permission of John Wiley & Sons, Inc.

formation. Some Internet experts believe that more people now use the Net for health information than for shopping or pornography.

Across the country, doctors report that when they tell a patient that he or she has a serious disease, more often than not, the patient goes home, cranks up a favorite Web search engine, and looks up the condition. Huge amounts of data about treatment, symptoms, and diagnosis are available—some good, some not good at all. If the patient doesn't personally look up the condition on the Web, then a child, spouse, niece, nephew, cousin, grandchild, coworker, or neighbor generally will do it for him or her.

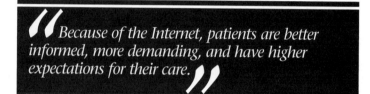

Because of the Internet, patients are better informed, more demanding, and have higher expectations for their care.

Then when the patient reenters the doctor's office for that first postdiagnosis visit, the scenario is very different from what it would have been only two or three years ago. Back then, a patient with a dread disease or complex condition came to the doctor's office humbly hoping that the all-knowing and hopefully all-powerful physician could explain the medical condition and plot out a cure. The doctor was the sole source of relevant knowledge and, in almost all cases, the sole source of medical strategy.

The physician would define the condition and then tell the patient what the preferred treatment "should" be. Patients would tell their friends, "Dr. Jones says I should be operated on next week. Boy, I'm sure glad I have her for a doctor." The doctor's words, in that pre-Web interaction, were gold.

Today, thanks to the Internet, the patient often returns to the exam room bearing an armful of Internet printouts and remarkably well informed about the disease and eager to discuss care alternatives. That's a revolutionary change in the caregiver-patient relationship. It is incredibly empowering for the patient. Medical issues are no longer purely medical mysteries resolved only by all-powerful, all-knowing medical gurus. Physicians are still highly respected and powerful gurus, but they are no longer the only gurus in the game. . . .

Better-informed patients are more demanding. Patients no longer passively accept whatever treatments their physicians recommend. Instead, they increasingly feel as if they are partners in their own care, able to understand care alternatives and express preferences.

As a side note, this change in roles has been a difficult adjustment for many older physicians. Some do not like feeling challenged by patients. One well-known doctor in Minnesota told patients, "If you're going to get your diagnosis and treatment information on the Web, get your care off the Web too. Get out of my office. Go to the Web doctor for your care."

Fortunately, that perspective isn't held by many physicians. Some of the best and most enlightened medical schools are beginning to teach students how to use the new wealth of Web research done by patients as a useful and convenient extension of the doctors' own research efforts. Those schools teach the new physicians how to sort quickly through the patient's armload of Web printouts to find the ones that originate from credible sources and might contain useful information.

Most medical school students today come from the computer generation. They not only are comfortable with Web-based information; they expect it. It's hard to convince a student who has done research on the Web through high school and college to learn to use classical paper textbooks at medical school.

Web Sites Can Improve Care

This new Web involvement in care has two very different impacts on costs. On the one hand, the Web creates demanding patients. On the other hand, the Web has the potential to enhance the effectiveness of physicians.

Knowledgeable patients are quite often more demanding patients. Some medical conditions are relatively rare. Physicians may see them only infrequently, if at all. Conditions such as muscular dystrophy, cancer of the rectum, gout, and chronic renal failure tend to be less than 1 percent of a given primary care doctor's practice. In other words, many doctors have traditionally treated relatively infrequently seen conditions even though those conditions are not part of the doctor's daily patient load and even though each doctor's personal knowledge about the most effective and successful current practices for these rare diseases may not be entirely up to date.

Some doctors do a magnificent job of caring for those patients. Others do less well. No one knows which doctors do what. What we do know is that treatments for those conditions vary widely from town to town, practice to practice, and doctor to doctor. In one study, 135 doctors who were all given the same patient example came up with eighty-two different treatments.

Patients Seek Information on the Web

Patients start out with a very limited overall array of medical knowledge. That now often changes when patients learn that they have an alarming diagnosis. For the most part, patients with a serious medical issue quickly begin to seek information about their condition. That makes obvious sense. From the patient's perspective, the statistical ratios relative to the frequency of the disease work in direct contrast to the physician's ratios. In other words, a given medical condition may make up only one-half of 1 percent of a given physician's practice, but for a patient who suffers personally from that particular condition, that diagnosis represents 100 percent of the patient's medical status. That personal focus gives the patient a huge incentive to become at least a lay expert on that one disease.

As patients become Web-trained "experts," quite often they start suggesting care options to the doctor. Those care options may involve expensive drugs, expensive specialty referrals, or expensive medical procedures. Patients sometimes know where the best new research on their disease is being done before their doctors even know that the new research exists.

For the most part, the result is better care. It never hurts any physician to get the most current medical information about a given condition. Web printouts can help.

Web Sites Can Also Lead to Bad Care

Unfortunately, however, not all information on the Web is accurate. Some is glaringly, even dangerously, inaccurate. That can create real problems, particularly when the Web sites seem credible to the patient. There are no standards for inclusion on the Internet. Anyone can offer health advice on the Web. There's no screening process for determining who is an appropriately trained and licensed source of Web information and who is a crackpot. Reeducating misled patients can and does waste a lot

54

of doctors' valuable energy and time, adding to the cost of care.

Another Web issue relates back to that persistent problem area of "unproven" care. Complications arise between patients and doctors and patients and plans when the care suggestions that the patient found on the Internet involve untried, unproven, currently experimental care. Recall that most experimental care isn't covered by insurance. Some highly subjective Web sites can make various kinds of untested care sound wonderful and successful beyond belief. Anecdotes abound, and in most of those anecdotes, miracles happen. Those anecdotes don't have to be accurate to be influential; they just need to be available. The Web makes them available.

Patients with serious illnesses who learn about supposedly promising experimental programs in distant medical research centers can sometimes put huge pressure on their local doctor to refer them to such centers. These patients can also put pressure on their health plan to pay for the care if they are treated in such centers. In those sad instances where the patient's prognosis is extremely poor with standard treatment and the research is being done by credible scientists, there is often a powerful and totally logical pressure exerted by patients who believe those programs give them their only chance of success—maybe their only chance of living. . . .

The Web has the potential to enhance the effectiveness of physicians.

It's absolutely easy to understand the patient's perspective. If a person is dying of cancer or some other dread disease and has been told by the doctor that death is inevitable, then any care alternative that seems to promise even a 1 percent chance of survival can look pretty good.

Most people are not actuaries or mathematicians. A 1 percent chance of survival becomes translated and reinterpreted in the minds of most people to actually mean "chance versus no chance" or "choice versus no choice," or, in a nutshell, "hope versus no hope."

That yes/no, hope/no hope context feels emotionally like fifty-fifty or even 100 percent (a chance) versus zero (no chance). People want a chance. They want a chance to live. They want a chance for their child to walk or talk. One percent is an important, context-setting, and numerically weighted decision factor for a mathematician. It's the only hope for the parent of a dying child.

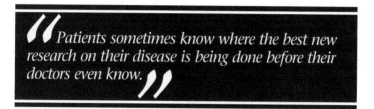

Patients sometimes know where the best new research on their disease is being done before their doctors even know.

As those payout patterns grow and experimental care becomes a more common expense for health plans, insurers, and various government programs, we can expect a further increase in the rate of health care cost growth. Many of those experiments can be extremely expensive. One experimental program for autistic children was priced at $500,000 per child. That might be a reasonable price if the program had been proven in vigorous clinical trials to work. It's a lot of money to pay for an unproven experiment. But because it was featured on a Web site, it created a lot of pressure with some understandably frustrated parents of autistic children.

In 2000, the United States spent nearly $4.5 billion on various kinds of clinical trials. More than 80 percent of this spending came from biotechnology, medical device, and pharmaceutical companies. If the trend continues, the amount of money spent on clinical trials and experimental care will continue to climb, keeping the rate of increase in research costs at an all-time-high level.

As each new procedure, technology, and treatment is shown to work, that information will be widely communicated over the Internet, and patient expectations will continue to work in favor of ever more expensive care. The American philosophy of health is, "When it works, we use it—and insurance pays for it." That philosophy is strongly supported by the existence of the Web.

Physicians Benefit from the Web

An even more exciting use of the Web relates to having a wide array of scientific knowledge and data about medical best practices available to the actual physician or other caregivers. Physicians traditionally have had to hunt down their own scientific updates through what is often a relatively haphazard process that includes seminars, journal articles, and salespeople from drug companies and medical equipment manufacturers. We are now moving beyond that point to having search engines for physicians that can do a much more thorough, complete, and timely review of the available source and literature for individual patients. In the very best settings, that information is available to the physician on a computer screen in the exam room, as well as being available for more complete review later in the privacy of the physician's office.

The best systems not only bring that information to the physician. They also create instant printouts for patients showing the exact nature of their disease and the appropriate next steps for dealing with it. . . .

The Net Delivers More Care

The Internet is more than a library. It can also be used to deliver care. The use of the Net for care delivery will grow dramatically over the next several years. Direct Net consultations from medical experts will become common. Perhaps a third of current office visits will become unnecessary, replaced by far more convenient Web contacts. House calls, that is, virtual house calls, will return for a great many patients. Visual linkages will enable doctors to see patients in their homes, and technology in the home will be able to provide weight, pulse, temperature, and blood pressure information and even, for selected patients with specific diseases, blood chemistry and selected lab test reports.

How will these developments affect the cost of care?

Done well, they could both improve care and reduce the costs of care. They should, at a minimum, significantly improve patient access to certain kinds of care. Web cams will allow for middle-of-the-night "face-to-face" consultations that would otherwise require inconvenient and even wasteful trips to urgent care or emergency settings. Follow-up care is particularly amenable to Web interactions.

There is, however, a major obstacle in place right now to Web-based medicine: providers won't do it if they can't get paid for it. Right now, most insurers do not pay for Web-based care. Insurers need to learn how to pay for those types of services. Some form of charge structure has to be created. Most

Web care now is not reimbursed by insurers, self-insured employers, or government programs. Why not? In part, because of the fear that costs will explode if Web-based care is available. Some payers are afraid that greedy revenue-seeking providers might decide, for example, that their chronic care patients all need two or three billable extra "Web consults" a week rather than one billable face-to-face consult every two weeks.

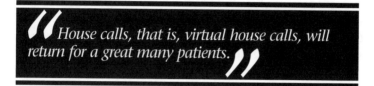

House calls, that is, virtual house calls, will return for a great many patients.

Payers worry that patients will find Web access to their own doctor so convenient and even pleasant that they will seek Web care constantly for very minor care issues. Hypochondriacs could find access to their physician only two Web clicks away. Every day. Likewise, some people just like attention, especially caregiver attention.

The problem could be a particular challenge for Medicare patients. For seniors with transportation problems, Web-based interaction with their caregivers could be a real blessing. But contact might become too easy. How many Medicare patients will take advantage of the opportunity to discuss their health issues daily? How many lonely older folks will use the Web and their doctor as a way of having contact with someone who cares? What will all of that contact cost? . . .

Patients want Web care now. Web care and e-visits both make immense sense. They can make care easier and more convenient for millions of patients. Those developments represent the next major service enhancement for care delivery. In multispecialty medical groups like the ones we work for, the uses of that tool are obvious and compelling. The challenge will be to resolve all of the relevant issues in a way that creates the best and most convenient care for patients while paying providers fairly for their time and expertise.

In health plans where the care system is exclusively part of the overall plan, many of the fee-for-service e-visit issues disappear. Plans like Group Health of Puget Sound, Kaiser Permanente, and HealthPartners will probably be pioneers in delivering care over the Net, in part because they work with salaried physicians, not just with fee-based physicians.

Long-Distance Care

Another nice feature of the Net is that it makes distances disappear. Web care can be done continents away. A patient who has a heart attack in Spain may be able—with the right system—to have his complete medical record sent in seconds from his U.S. doctor to his Spanish caregiver.

Long-distance care will soon become a way of having the best providers in America (Mayo Clinic) able to provide specialty consultations in other countries or even in other regions of this country. The good news is that that level of specialty service could restore competition for some services in certain otherwise monopolistic markets. The bad news is that local providers in many markets are seeking to use local licensing laws to prevent use of that level of Internet care.

In any case, the Web is transforming care. Up to this point, the primary impact has been to add expense. Over time, that impact may change. More consistent care may reduce the costly complications that result from less-than-optimal care. In either case, care has already improved. And "we ain't seen nothing yet."

8

The Internet Puts Patients at Risk

David Hasemyer

David Hasemyer is a staff writer for the San Diego Union-Tribune.

Some doctors are prescribing potentially lethal drugs over the Internet without examining their patients. These patients sometimes become addicted, commit suicide, or overdose from the medications. While some states have made prescribing drugs over the Internet illegal, no federal law prohibits the practice even though the medical community believes it is a serious threat to the public's health. State regulators have difficulty finding and prosecuting these doctors, and budget restrictions in some states make the task even more difficult. Without state and federal backing, prosecutors will have an impossible job shutting down the doctors who prescribe dangerous medications over the Internet.

From her nondescript office in a strip mall on Paradise Valley Road [in Spring Valley, California], Dr. Dianna Norman prescribed potentially deadly doses of stimulants and other powerful drugs to people she had never seen, much less examined.

Sitting at her computer, she used the Internet to prescribe hundreds of thousands of pills to people from Minnesota to Florida. For $99 a month, court records show they could buy a supply of Phentermine, Xenical or Meridia—addictive weight-loss pills.

The only "examination" Norman performed on her cyber

patients was instructing them to fill out a questionnaire about their medical history. "Please be truthful," the online registration form urged.

Cyber doctors throughout the United States are prescribing drugs for people who sometimes get hooked on them, try to commit suicide with them or, increasingly, overdose and die on them.

The 2001 death of Ryan Thomas Haight, an 18-year-old from La Mesa [California], has been connected to prescriptions filled via the Internet. So has the April [2003] death of a 47-year-old Sacramento man.

"You send in the money, they send out the drugs. That's all there is to it," said Nancy Harler a South Carolina nurse who was hooked on narcotic pain medication and fed her addiction with pills prescribed over the Internet by a San Bernardino County [California] doctor.

A Lack of Resources

The ease with which Internet prescriptions are written and filled—and the lack of government resources to control the practice—has state regulators across the country worried that more people will die. "From our perspective, Internet prescribing has become one of the biggest threats to public safety," said Dr. James N. Thompson, president of the Federation of State Medical Boards, which represents 70 medical and licensing boards across the country.

There are no federal laws to regulate Internet prescribing and no way of knowing how many doctors are doing business online or how many customers they are attracting. So far 28 states, including California, have passed legislation regulating the practice. The California law states, in essence, that doctors must physically examine their patients before prescribing medication.

Some states are overwhelmed by the task of penetrating the layers of cyberspace that shield doctors. Kristine Smith, spokeswoman for the New York State Department of Health, said her agency hasn't even begun to craft rules for the Internet, because "it's almost impossible to find the doctors doing this."

As frustrated authorities scramble to police the Internet, doctors continue to set up cyber offices where they e-mail prescriptions to anyone with a credit card and a self-diagnosis. "Rather than see three patients in one hour, a doctor can sit on the Internet and prescribe to 600 people in an hour and make a lot more money," said Dr. Hazem Chehabi, president of the California medical board.

An Impossible Task

Since California's law went into effect in 2001, 12 California doctors have had their licenses revoked or faced other discipline for prescribing over the Internet. The medical board also has fined six out-of-state doctors millions of dollars for prescribing to Californians.

Since June [2003], however, the board's job has become more difficult. That's when it lost its only investigator dedicated to tracking cyber doctors. Paul Nasca, a former Sacramento cop with degrees in genetics and biology, nabbed 24 doctors—some whose cases are pending—in the two years he held the job.

But when Nasca left for a higher-paying job, the board couldn't replace him because of a state hiring freeze. Board officials acknowledge that catching cyber doctors is now more likely to happen by chance than by investigative scrutiny.

Shutting down every doctor who prescribes over the Internet is an impossible task, said Ron Joseph, the medical board's executive director. There are simply too many of them and too few investigators to go after them. "We can't come close to getting them all," Joseph said.

Other states also are scrambling for money to fund cyber investigations, which can be painstakingly slow and sometimes fruitless. "States have to get the most bang for their bucks," said Dale L. Austin, chief operating officer for the Federation of State Medical Boards. "It's like looking for a needle in a haystack," Austin said. "So state boards are putting their resources into investigations that yield more results."

A Doctor Is Caught

Authorities stumbled onto Dianna Norman's Internet doctoring during a routine review of U.S. Drug Enforcement Administration [DEA] records covering drug purchases by doctors in 1999.

They found that the South Bay Terraces [a suburb of San Diego, California] doctor was buying enough weight-loss drugs to qualify as a distributor, according to a medical board accusation filed in administrative law court here. They also discovered that Norman, who has been licensed to practice medicine in California since 1981, had a Web site offering diet drugs for sale. The DEA notified the medical board and launched a sting.

An investigator rented mailboxes in Valley Center, Holtville and Santa Ysabel under different names. Then she went online and filled out the doctor's questionnaire. On some of the forms, the investigator listed a weight that clearly indicated she was not obese and therefore not a suitable patient. On other forms, she indicated she was taking drugs that would have a deadly reaction if mixed with the drugs Norman was prescribing.

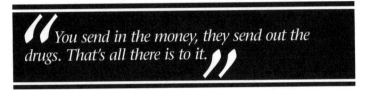

You send in the money, they send out the drugs. That's all there is to it.

Norman sent the drugs anyway. When the DEA searched her office and home, they found nearly 2,000 charts. One 89-pound drug addict told investigators that Norman had sent her Phentermine, an amphetamine-like drug used for weight loss.

Through her lawyer, Norman, who is 50, declined a request to discuss the case. "She wants to put this behind her and get on with her life, and talking about it further stirs up the emotions," attorney Keith Greer said.

Instead of facing a hearing, Norman agreed last year [in 2002] to a two-month suspension of her license, five years' probation and an assessment of her medical skills. She'll also have to take an ethics course and a medical refresher course on prescribing.

Two Crucial Questions

The anonymous cloak of the Internet raises two crucial questions: Are the doctors who they say they are? And do their patients really need the drugs?

Doctors "need to know if they are prescribing Viagra to a 17-year-old boy or Phentermine to a 120-pound woman looking for an amphetamine rush," said San Diego–based Deputy Attorney General Mary Agnes Matyszewski, one of four lawyers statewide who handle Internet prosecutions for the medical board. "They have no idea."

Dr. Jim Knight, president of the San Diego Medical Society,

said patients seeking medical help from a computer instead of in a doctor's office take an even bigger risk because they can't verify the credentials of the person who is writing the prescription. If a doctor doesn't fully understand a patient's illness and medical history, the drugs being prescribed could have deadly interactions with other medications or aggravate existing medical conditions.

Dr. Steve Green, chairman of family practice at Sharp Rees-Stealy [medical group], used the example of a man getting Viagra without a physical exam. What seems to be a sexual problem could actually be a sign of a pituitary tumor or of high blood pressure, he said. "Letting people do these things outside of a clinical setting—no matter if the motivation for the patients is to save time and money—is potentially dangerous," Knight said. "You're really blind on the Internet."

Feeding Addictions

Cyber doctors ignore medicine's basic principles: to know their patients and do them no harm.

Dr. Jon Opsahl, a San Bernardino County doctor who prescribed to Nancy Harler, Amanda Bridges and Barbara Benoit, neither knew his patients nor cared about them, state medical officials said in the accusation that led to the revocation of his license in February [2003].

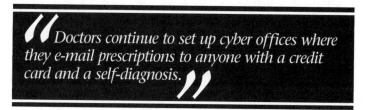

Doctors continue to set up cyber offices where they e-mail prescriptions to anyone with a credit card and a self-diagnosis.

Harler turned to the Internet two years ago [in 2001] after her family doctor refused to continue prescribing Lortab, an addictive painkiller, for her arthritis. With just a few keystrokes and a Google search, she found Opsahl. Getting him to prescribe Lortab was easy, she said. "I could have said anything (on the questionnaire). The doctor had no way of knowing," Harler said in an interview from her home in Columbia, S.C. "The only thing he asked was how many do you want."

Opsahl fed Harler's escalating addiction from his office in Colton [California], 2,000 miles away. An Internet pharmacy filled the prescriptions from Las Vegas. Harler introduced her daughter, Bridges, to the Web site, and soon Opsahl was prescribing Lortab to both mother and daughter, according to court records.

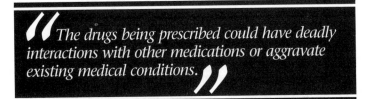

The drugs being prescribed could have deadly interactions with other medications or aggravate existing medical conditions.

At one point, Opsahl agreed with Harler that she needed to reduce her dependence on the drug, and Harler decided to quit. But she continued getting Lortab for her daughter, according to her declaration filed with an administrative law judge. Eventually, Harler said she realized her daughter's life was being ruined by the narcotics and asked Opsahl to wean Bridges from the drugs. "I . . . was surprised when she informed me that Dr. Opsahl continued to fax new prescriptions for her even when he was aware of her addiction," Harler said in her declaration. "We are a good family, but we got caught up in this mess before knowing how devastating it could be," Harler wrote to Opsahl.

When Benoit hooked up with Opsahl last year, she was looking for someone to feed her addiction to the narcotic sleep aid Temazepam. Opsahl didn't ask much about her medical history, and Benoit told him only that she had trouble sleeping and was in pain from a back injury. "It was pretty simple," Benoit said in a telephone interview from her home in Wisconsin.

Benoit, 47, can't remember the day she almost died, but the details are preserved in police reports. Her father found her in a stupor, so sedated she couldn't control her bodily functions or tell paramedics how many pills she had taken. The instructions on the prescription she had obtained a couple of days earlier said to take one tablet a day for insomnia. But police reports stated that she had swallowed as many as 28 of the maroon and blue capsules. Benoit, who was hospitalized for several days, said her addiction is now under control.

Another Doctor Prosecuted

Opsahl came to the attention of the California medical board's Internet investigator shortly after the Sept. 11, 2001, terrorist attacks, when he used the Internet to sell Cipro, an antibiotic that is effective against anthrax.

He later linked up with the Internet site "Office in a Snap," which he used to prescribe the painkiller Vicodin and anxiety reducers Valium and Xanax.

Opsahl also operated another Web site, which he used to draw attention to his mother's murder in 1975. Myrna Opsahl was shot to death in Sacramento [California] during a failed bank robbery by the Symbionese Liberation Army.[1]

According to the medical board, Opsahl "repeatedly prescribed excess quantities of dangerous drugs" to 2,300 Internet patients in 2001 and 2002. In an interview with *The San Diego Union-Tribune* from his office, Opsahl insisted that Internet medicine poses no risk to patients as long as they are being treated for a limited number of pre-existing disorders such as chronic pain. "For some patients it's not in their best interests to turn to the Internet," he said. "But for others, let's make medicine convenient and available."

Although Opsahl, 43, didn't examine his patients, he told the medical board that he reviewed their medical records and talked with those who had previously diagnosed problems. In a declaration filed in court, he said "no actual harm was caused to these patients by my actions."

"When it comes down to it, if a patient lies to you and denies that they are an addict and wants these meds, it's on them," Opsahl told the medical board through his lawyer. "It's their responsibility. What am I supposed to be, a mind reader? Even if I met them in my office, they might lie to me. So what's the difference?" Opsahl told *The Union-Tribune* he stands by that statement. "It sounds callous and uncaring, but that is how I feel," he said.

In February [2004], the medical board stripped Opsahl of his medical license, and he now works as a sports medicine consultant. The investigation that resulted in his punishment was led by Paul Nasca, the former cyber detective whose job with the California medical board remains unfilled.

---

1. The Symbionese Liberation Army (SLA) was a terrorist group based in the United States that committed two murders in the early 1970s.

9

The Internet Has Not Changed Politics

David Lytel

David Lytel was codeveloper of the White House Web site when he served in the White House Office of Science and Technology Policy in the first Clinton administration. He is cofounder and managing partner of Democrats.com, which provides Internet campaign services for candidates and committees.

Although some people in the last few presidential elections believed that the Internet would revolutionize politics, that result has yet to materialize. One of the reasons is that there are still not enough people online. Also, some argue that because the Internet is still not capable of delivering video to most users, it is not as powerful for political campaigns as television. However, the biggest reason the Internet has not become a greater campaign tool is campaign managers. They do not expect much from the Internet and so put little effort and money into it. Conversely, some managers expect the Internet to be a miracle fund-raising tool without making the necessary efforts to make it effective. In addition, they do not understand their audience and are not creative in developing Web site content. Finally, those who currently run political campaigns have little experience with the Internet medium and are unsure how to manage it. Once changes are made to correct these problems, the Internet will have the potential to change politics.

In the year before each of the last three national elections, speculation has run rampant that perhaps this would be the

David Lytel, "The Wire Next Time: Rethinking the Internet's Place in Politics," *Campaigns & Elections*, June 2002, p. 56. Copyright © 2002 by Campaigns & Elections, Inc. Reproduced by permission.

year that the Internet would revolutionize politics. Thanks to widespread use of the Internet, the story goes, candidates would be more responsive to the public, political dialogue would engage the nonvoters, and the political system would become more transparent. All of this would usher in a new era of dynamic, citizen-centered political conversation.

Then, after each election, an uncomfortable reality once again asserts itself, The campaigns, corporations and foundations that have collectively spent millions on the Internet quietly pull the plug on their ventures, vowing never to make the same mistakes again—at least until next time, which will almost surely be the Year the Internet will Transform Politics.

The interpretation of what went wrong almost always focuses on two easy things to measure—the number of Internet users and the still-limited bandwidth available to most subscribers.

There just aren't enough people online yet, some argue, and that's why Internet politics has been a disappointment so far. Once the Internet reaches as many households as television then surely the revolution will come, says this theory. But already the Internet reaches almost the entire half of the U.S. population that votes in elections. And among the unwired, there is a strong correlation between disinterest in the Internet and disinterest in politics.

The other common argument is that the Internet just isn't powerful enough yet. People may not want to read text, but when the broadband Internet arrives and can deliver video, then surely the revolution will come. But television works because the advertisements wash over you, often too quickly to change the channel. Very little that actually commands your attention comes to you passively on the Internet. There is no medium that's ever been more powerful for screening out stuff you don't want to see, and political commercials fall into that category for most people.

While both these observations are true—of course the Internet would be more important for politics if it had a bigger audience and was more visual and easier to use—neither really explains the lack of a mass audience for politics on the Internet.

The Internet's Misuse in Politics

I've been doing interactive media and political communication since before there was an Internet. My doctoral research was on how a rudimentary precursor to the Internet called Minitel was used by French voters and parties in the French legislative and presidential elections of 1986 and 1988. From that work and the experience of providing Internet campaign services for several dozen candidates and committees via Democrats.com, here is my list of the top 10 reasons why the Internet cannot yet claim to have changed the results of any elections, and what it will take to have a breakthrough.

10. Low expectations. Once the Web site works, most campaign managers want their Internet consultant to go away. Campaign managers are generally satisfied if they get a press hit about the release of their Web site, and figure that if they ever hear about their Web site again during the campaign it will probably be bad news. Expectations for what you can do with Internet campaigning, in other words, are set so low that we don't really even get the chance to show what we can do.

9. High expectations. The expectations of campaign fundraisers, however, have been excessive because so many of them bought the illusion that people spontaneously race to their computers in a mad rush to send their money to candidates. Admittedly there are fewer and fewer who believe in this magical get-rich-quick miracle, which was born out of the myth of the John McCain presidential campaign's fundraising experience.

The McCain campaign did not, as has been widely reported, reap a windfall in spontaneous online contributions after his victory in the New Hampshire primary [in 2000]. Rather, his organization was so rudimentary that his staff and volunteers used their own Web site as a distributed electronic cash register, and entered the credit card numbers of their supporters into the Web site as a way of collecting contributions when they responded positively to an outbound telemarketing call.

There is, of course, money to be raised on the Internet but it involves the much slower and methodical work of building sizable e-mail lists and then cultivating these people over time.

8. Misunderstanding the audience. Some candidates and campaign managers believe Internet users are lunatics. In March 2002, NBC's "West Wing" acknowledged the existence of the Internet for the first time—but only to portray the denizens of "LemonLyman.com" as crazies who were not to be seriously engaged. In reality, the 50 percent of Americans who use the Internet are pretty much the same 50 percent who vote. And unlike video zombies, Internet users are awake, alert, and want to have a say in the world they live in.

7. Lack of creativity. When we get some of the candidate's

time for Internet stuff we squander it. Online politics still gets reduced to real-time online "chats" with political celebrities, which is almost as boring to participate in as it is to watch.

Campaign managers now understand that they can reach a larger audience during just one day on any licensed radio station in the country than they can by doing a live chat session on even the largest online service. But we seldom give campaigns anything to do with candidates on the Internet besides produce a live chat session, and campaigns almost never use the tactic that has been proven to launch effective viral marketing campaigns—humor, in the form of games, cartoons, jokes and other materials that make people laugh.

6. Too few campaigns publish a readable campaign newsletter. The method of Internet-enabled campaigning that has been proven to work is the publication of a regular electronic newsletter mixed with occasional requests for financial support.

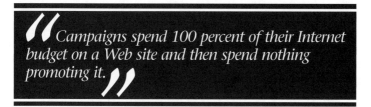

Campaigns spend 100 percent of their Internet budget on a Web site and then spend nothing promoting it.

But in many cases candidates and fundraisers are in such a hurry that they simply blast the hell out of the lists with repeated overt solicitations for funds while the lists are still small. Not surprisingly, people unsubscribe from them in droves rather than subject themselves to a barrage of requests for contributions. When people do receive a newsletter they think is valuable, not only do they contribute but they also forward the newsletter to their friends.

5. The only list-building activity most campaigns engage in is operating a Web site. The metrics of success with a Web site are amazingly simple. A good Web site is a good e-mail address collection machine and a bad Web site is a bad e-mail address collection machine.

Most campaigns don't use any method for creating sizable e-mail lists besides the conversion of ambient Web traffic to newsletter sign-ups. Since a campaign is doing great if it has a 5 percent conversion rate and traffic on campaign Web sites is never very high, this method almost never creates lists of sufficient size to have an impact either on the campaign or on the election.

4. Campaigns spend 100 percent of their Internet budget on a Web site and then spend nothing promoting it. Think of the motion picture industry. In the 1940s, a film's budget was almost entirely the cost of producing it. Since there was a ready audience going to the movies regularly, the studio didn't have to do much more than print up a poster to display. By the 1970s, however, there was so much competition for the consumer's entertainment dollars and so many films that production and promotional budgets were roughly equal. Today, of course, the promotional budgets are an order of magnitude larger than even the most elaborately overblown production budgets.

It takes money to break through the incredibly noisy message environment so that a film can find its audience. In the commercial Internet world, no one believes that they can just build a Web site and sit back and wait for people to find it.

Campaign managers don't tell candidates to rent an office and stand in the doorway waiting for voters to wander by, but that is exactly what most campaigns do with their Web site. Instead, being successful means going out and finding voters and supporters, just like with every other medium used in campaigning.

3. Campaigns almost never give their Internet presence the level of effort required for it to succeed by keeping their site regularly updated, animated and alive. If a campaign manages to scrounge up a little bit of money to get on the air with one television spot that airs two times the weekend before the election, would anyone think that television had been tried and failed? No, we'd all agree that the campaign simply didn't do enough paid media to have any impact. So it is with the Internet. Since the sites are infrequently updated, not promoted and little effort is made to build lists, the Web sites mostly just sit there, like a car waiting to be taken out for a drive.

2. The media consultants don't get their cut of a campaign's Internet expenditures, and keep Internet expenditures to a minimum. Media consultants have for the most part figured out that having an Internet address in the last few frames of a television commercial helps legitimize the claims contained in the ad. But the "Web site" they want consists of a few lines of text citing the ad's sources. The media consultants have a vested interest in sucking all of the campaign's expenditures into their domain because they get paid a percentage of the campaign's advertising budget.

1. The rules for being successful in an interactive medium are heretical to people trained to understand the reality of the broadcast regime. The biggest obstacle to getting campaign decision-makers to authorize serious online organizing is that it requires that they suspend the cardinal rule for all political professionals who have come of age in the era of the television-centered campaign—that effective, modern campaign management is about message control.

The Internet is most effective as a campaign medium when a campaign's strong partisans can be harnessed to carry on a sustained conversation with its weak partisans, so that they become sufficiently engaged to actually get out and vote. (Undecided voters, of course, already have the perfect medium to help convince them. It is called television and we should let it do its job.) To create this dynamic means, the vote hunters have to do something really counterintuitive and difficult for them—they have to hand the rifle over to the deer. That's right, actually distribute firearms with live rounds so that the prey can help hunt other prey.

To a campaign manager this is very scary. It is a whole lot less risky to spend the money on messages that the campaign can control. We all know that monologues are incredibly boring interactive programming. They just don't work online. But most campaigns and most campaign Web sites are paid monologues.

In fact, there are a handful of campaigns using good, tested permission-based marketing techniques and pay-per-action advertising to build their lists. A few of these will be the first to build lists of unprecedented scale and generate the kind of impact that so far the Internet has not achieved.

[In the future], in the White House, Congress, or maybe a governor's mansion there will be a politician who got the Internet very right in his or her campaign who will turn to his aides, as John F. Kennedy did after the 1960 election pointing to a television set, and say "we wouldn't have won without that thing." That will be the year the Internet will have come of age as a political medium.

10

Businesses and Consumers Benefit from the Internet

Paul Markillie

Paul Markillie writes for the Economist *in London, England.*

Internet business is booming. Billions of dollars are now being spent on Web sites that offer travel, medications, books, and many more products for both business and individual customers. The Internet influences consumer purchases offline as well because customers research items such as automobiles and appliances on the Internet before buying at stores. As a result, Web sites are powerful tools for businesses to attract and keep customers. Some believe that many stores will eventually become just showrooms for customers who buy online. The combination of low cost and convenience will continue to attract customers to the Internet.

When the technology bubble burst in 2000, the crazy valuations for online companies vanished with it, and many businesses folded. The survivors plugged on as best they could, encouraged by the growing number of internet users. Now valuations are rising again and some of the dotcoms are making real profits, but the business world has become much more cautious about the internet's potential. The funny thing is that the wild predictions made at the height of the boom—namely, that vast chunks of the world economy would move into cyberspace—are, in one way or another, coming true.

The raw numbers tell only part of the story. According to America's Department of Commerce, online retail sales in the world's biggest market last year [in 2003] rose by 26%, to $55 billion. That sounds like a lot of money, but it amounts to only 1.6% of total retail sales. The vast majority of people still buy most things in the good old "bricks-and-mortar" world.

But the commerce department's figures deal with only part of the retail industry. For instance, they exclude online travel services, one of the most successful and fastest-growing sectors of e-commerce. InterActiveCorp (IAC), the owner of expedia.com and hotels.com, alone sold $10 billion–worth of travel last year [in 2003]—and it has plenty of competition, not least from airlines, hotels and car-rental companies, all of which increasingly sell online.

Nor do the figures take in things like financial services, ticket-sales agencies, pornography (a $2 billion business in America last year [in 2003], according to Adult Video News, a trade magazine), online dating and a host of other activities, from tracing ancestors to gambling (worth perhaps $6 billion worldwide). They also leave out purchases in grey markets, such as the online pharmacies that are thought to be responsible for a good proportion of the $700 [million] that Americans spent last year on buying cut-price prescription drugs from across the border in Canada.

Tip of the Iceberg

And there is more. The commerce department's figures include the fees earned by internet auction sites, but not the value of goods that are sold: an astonishing $24 billion–worth of trade was done last year on eBay, the biggest online auctioneer. Nor, by definition, do they include the billions of dollars–worth of goods bought and sold by businesses connecting to each other over the internet. Some of these B2B [business to business] services are proprietary; for example, Wal-Mart tells its suppliers that they must use its own system if they want to be part of its annual turnover of $250 billion.

So e-commerce is already very big, and it is going to get much bigger. But the actual value of transactions currently concluded online is dwarfed by the extraordinary influence the internet is exerting over purchases carried out in the offline world. That influence is becoming an integral part of e-commerce.

To start with, the internet is profoundly changing consumer behaviour. One in five customers walking into a Sears department store in America to buy an electrical appliance will have researched their purchase online—and most will know down to a dime what they intend to pay. More surprisingly, three out of four Americans start shopping for new cars online, even though most end up buying them from traditional dealers. The difference is that these customers come to the showroom armed with information about the car and the best available deals. Sometimes they even have computer print-outs identifying the particular vehicle from the dealer's stock that they want to buy.

Half of the 60 [million] consumers in Europe who have an internet connection bought products offline after having investigated prices and details online, according to a study by Forrester, a research consultancy. Different countries have different habits. In Italy and Spain, for instance, people are twice as likely to buy offline as online after researching on the internet. But in Britain and Germany, the two most developed internet markets, the numbers are evenly split. Forrester says that people begin to shop online for simple, predictable products, such as DVDs, and then graduate to more complex items. Used-car sales are now one of the biggest online growth areas in America.

People seem to enjoy shopping on the internet, if high customer-satisfaction scores are any guide. Websites are doing ever more and cleverer things to serve and entertain their customers, and seem set to take a much bigger share of people's overall spending in the future.

Why Websites Matter

This has enormous implications for business. A company that neglects its website may be committing commercial suicide. A website is increasingly becoming the gateway to a company's brand, products and services—even if the firm does not sell online. A useless website suggests a useless company, and a rival is only a mouse-click away. But even the coolest website will be lost in cyberspace if people cannot find it, so companies have to ensure that they appear high up in internet search results.

For many users, a search site is now their point of entry to the internet. The best-known search engine has already entered the lexicon: people say they have "Googled" a company, a product or their plumber. The search business has also developed one of the most effective forms of advertising on the internet. And it is already the best way to reach some consumers: teenagers and young men spend more time online than watching television. All this means that search is turning into the internet's next big battleground as Google defends itself against challenges from [search engines] Yahoo! and Microsoft.

The other way to get noticed online is to offer goods and services through one of the big sites that already get a lot of traffic. EBay, Yahoo! and Amazon are becoming huge trading platforms for other companies. But to take part, a company's products have to stand up to intense price competition. People check online prices, compare them with those in their local high street and may well take a peek at what customers in other countries are paying. Even if websites are prevented from shipping their goods abroad, there are plenty of web-based entrepreneurs ready to oblige.

A company that neglects its website may be committing commercial suicide.

What is going on here is arbitrage between different sales channels, says Mohanbir Sawhney, professor of technology at the Kellogg School of Management in Chicago. For instance, someone might use the internet to research digital cameras, but visit a photographic shop for a hands-on demonstration. "I'll think about it," they will tell the sales assistant. Back home, they will use a search engine to find the lowest price and buy online. In this way, consumers are "deconstructing the purchasing process", says Professor Sawhney. They are unbundling product information from the transaction itself.

It is not only price transparency that makes internet consumers so powerful; it is also the way the net makes it easy for them to be fickle. If they do not like a website, they swiftly move on. "The web is the most selfish environment in the world," says Daniel Rosensweig, chief operating officer of Yahoo! "People want to use the internet whenever they want, how they want and for whatever they want."

Yahoo! is not alone in defining its strategy as working out what its customers (260 [million] unique users every month) are looking for, and then trying to give it to them. The first thing they want is to become better informed about products and prices. "We operate our business on that belief," says Jeff Bezos, Amazon's chief executive. Amazon became famous for books, but long ago branched out into selling lots of other things too; among its latest ventures are health products, jewellery and gourmet food. Apart from cheap and bulky items such as garden rakes, Mr Bezos thinks he can sell most things. And so do the millions of people who use eBay.

And yet nobody thinks real shops are finished, especially those operating in niche markets. Many bricks-and-mortar bookshops still make a good living, as do flea markets. But many record shops and travel agents could be in for a tougher time. Erik Blachford, the head of IAC's travel site and boss of Expedia, the biggest internet travel agent, thinks online travel bookings in America could quickly move from 20% of the market to more than half. Mr Bezos reckons online retailers might capture 10–15% of retail sales over the next decade. That would represent a massive shift in spending.

How will traditional shops respond? Michael Dell, the founder of Dell, which leads the personal-computer market by selling direct to the customer, has long thought many shops will turn into showrooms There are already signs of change on the high street. The latest Apple and Sony stores are designed to display products, in the full expectation that many people will buy online. To some extent, the online and offline worlds may merge. Multi-channel selling could involve a combination of traditional shops, a printed catalogue, a home-shopping channel on TV, a phone-in order service and an e-commerce-enabled website. But often it is likely to be the website where customers will be encouraged to place their orders.

One of the biggest commercial advantages of the internet is a lowering of transaction costs, which usually translates directly into lower prices for the consumer. So, if the lowest prices can be found on the internet and people like the service they get, why would they buy anywhere else?

One reason may be convenience; another, concern about fraud, which poses the biggest threat to online trade. But as long as the internet continues to deliver price and product information quickly, cheaply and securely, e-commerce will continue to grow. Increasingly, companies will have to assume that customers will know exactly where to look for the best buy. This market has the potential to become as perfect as it gets.

11

The Benefits of Internet Business Are Overhyped

Martha Nichols

Martha Nichols is a contributing editor for the Women's Review of Books.

It is impossible to predict the future of Internet business because the Internet is developing and changing so quickly. The fortunes of companies involved with e-commerce are constantly rising and falling. The media has tended to focus on stories about entrepreneurs with dreams of conquering markets. However, beyond the hype, companies using the Internet as a tool still face the challenges of any business striving to be successful in a competitive market. Some e-businesses have yet to make a profit, pay their workers low wages, and are invading their customers' privacy with "cookies" that track customer online buying habits. Despite the challenges e-businesses face, Internet sales are increasing. Consumers can take advantage of some great deals as the Internet market establishes itself; however, they should beware of unscrupulous business practices.

How does the promise of the Internet match up to the reality?

You know that annoying Sock Puppet? This past November [2000], he lost his owner. Pets.com had attracted over half a million customers, but its growing sales couldn't keep up with losses, especially given the logistics of shipping a twenty-pound bag of dog food. No new investors or buyers stepped up to bail out the company. As CEO Jule Wainwright robotically explained in a press release: "With no better offers and avenues effectively exhausted, we felt that the best option was an orderly wind-down. . . ." Those who go to the Pets.com site are now funneled to Petsmart.com, a former competitor.

Even the few remaining Luddites[1] who avoid the Internet probably know that the dot-com bubble has burst. On its last day, Pets.com closed at 22 cents a share. F——edCompany.com (the name is a take-off on the rah-rah magazine *Fast Company*) maintains a running deathwatch on those that will be the next to fall. A sample posting on its home page for December 15, 2000: "It appears restaurant reservations site OpenTable.com has burned through cash faster than you can caramelize a creme brulee. Rumor has it they laid off about 40 employees— around 25%."

If e-business seems twisted, that's partly because of the Internet itself. It's a hybrid medium that began as a communications tool—a computer network originally funded through the US Department of Defense for use at universities—rather than as an electronic bourse or shopping mall. Now the Internet and World Wide Web serve many interests, including corporations, but they still traffic in information, a constantly evolving entity that slithers beyond conventional boundaries and is hard to quantify.

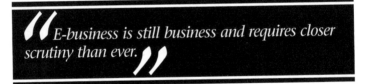

E-business is still business and requires closer scrutiny than ever.

Because the medium is so fluid, any discussion of where e-commerce is headed can only provide a snapshot in time; companies and stock prices ebb and flow as these words are typed. Still, it's important to separate the hype about the transformative potential of cyber-life—the kind of excess that fires up investors and pundits—from what's actually going on. So far, the media story has emphasized young entrepreneurs as swashbuckling heroes. Their tragic demise currently dominates the discussion, a sort of *House of Mirth*[2] for dudes in ponytails, who

1. Luddites are those who oppose technological change. 2. *House of Mirth* is a novel by Edith Wharton published in 1905 in which the main character is a woman whose only way of entering high society is to marry above her class.

thought they'd "marry up" in a corporate sale.

But the real story is far more complicated, a mix of over-ambitious dreamers, exploited employees, managers with no idea what they're doing and villains who often seem as innocuous as the Sock Puppet. In fact, the rapid growth of e-commerce shows just how well capitalism conforms to whatever comes its way. Once you scrape off the hype, at least two related points are clear: e-business reinforces the co-optation of everything for marketing purposes; and e-business is still business and requires closer scrutiny than ever.

The Story of Amazon.com

Take Amazon.com. The megillah of dot-coms, which opened in 1995, has yet to make a profit.[3] However, Amazon's sales topped $960 million in the fourth quarter of 2000 (up 42 percent from the same period in 1999), and it has a well-known brand, the *sine qua non* [absolutely essential] of millennial consumer business. To many Web customers, Amazon stands for convenience—from your computer to your front door in 24 hours—and vast selection. What's more, this brand drips with feel-good associations—books as the path to personal enlightenment and virtual community; books as the heart of a little-engine-that-could company that takes on the likes of Barnes & Noble. "We've all had books that have changed our lives," CEO and founder Jeff Bezos effusively claims, "and part of what we're doing at Amazon.com is trying to help you find and discover that next one."

The problem is the rest of what Amazon does. The company has made much of its special relationships with customers and the services like gift-wrapping that it provides, but in fact it has co-opted the language of independent booksellers. Amazon's site is easy to use and includes reviews from other customers, "Discussion Boards" about everything from authors to gardening, and "Purchase Circles" (a list of what other Amazon customers in Cambridge, Massachusetts, say, have bought). But building a community of buyers is what independents like feminist bookstores—particularly hard hit by the chains and online retailers—have done all along, and not just as a marketing ploy. In 1998, for example, Amazon.com was forced to admit that it had taken payments from publishers including Random House

---

3. Amazon.com has earned a profit as of 2004.

and Simon & Schuster, to list titles as "New and Notable" or to disguise gushing press releases as impartial reviews.

Then there are Amazon's thousands of workers, many of whom are stuck with boring, low-paying jobs. Although Amazon employees are supposed to be lured by the company's utopian ethos as well as stock options, customer-service workers have recently tried to unionize in Seattle. They are unhappy about low wages, the fluctuating share price, mandatory overtime and job security. Who can blame them, when Amazon has recently shifted some of its customer service via email to a contractor in India?

The company can no longer even claim that its books are cheaper. Originally, Amazon offered deep discounts, undercutting other booksellers even when shipping costs were added. But this past summer [of 2000], both Amazon and Barnesandnoble.com had to raise their online prices, caving in to the reality that book-selling is not a commodity business. This prompted one Harvard Square bookstore to hang a banner outside its front doors: "Thank you, Amazon.com for raising your prices! Sincerely, Wordsworth."

These shifts reveal what Jeff Bezos, who worked at a hedge fund before starting Amazon, has been up to all along: building a brand—books are an obvious hook for the Web's literate users—then expanding into other areas that pay off. Amazon.com now sells digital cameras, patio furniture, even foie gras. As Peter de Jonge noted in his scathing article; "Riding the Wild, Perilous Waters of Amazon.com" in the *New York Times Magazine* (March 14, 1999), "We may see that the grand vision for Amazon.com isn't much more than an electronic mall . . . and that Amazon.com's only real goal in regard to its customers, just like that of any other business, is to separate them from their money."

Online Sales

E-commerce as a whole is far from dead, but pundits can't help rehashing the obvious screw-ups. Buying pet food or toys or clothes by clicking through tiny pictures on a Web site still can't compete with paper catalogs or actual stores. Most regular users like you and me think Web banner ads are stupid. Earlier attempts to sell subscriptions to online magazine sites like Slate.com went nowhere; users just surfed until they found what they wanted for free. The dot-com players themselves cry that they need more time to build sales and word-of-mouth, that all companies lose money their first years out, especially if they're revolutionary. In practical terms, very few have come up with the right business model.

Yet while the current crop of dotcoms kills each other off, Internet sales are on the rise. In 1998, consumer spending on-line came to less than $10 billion; online sales for 2000 are likely to go over $35 billion. This is still a drop in the proverbial bucket for total retail sales: less than one percent of the take. (According to the US Census Bureau of the Department of Commerce, total retail sales for the third quarter of 2000 will be an estimated $812 billion; retail e-commerce sales will amount to just over $6 billion.) But the technical problems that have hindered growth so far will be ironed out. Typing in your credit-card number has become less scary. Computers, modems and cable systems will handle ever larger quantities of data at faster speeds. The dot-com retailers that survive will straighten our their problems with order fulfillment and customer returns.

One of the ironies of e-commerce . . . is that Old Economy companies have reaped the real benefits.

More important, e-business has warped beyond retail sales. Consider online transactions between businesses, which have benefited mega-corporations like DuPont, General Electric and American Airlines, to name but a few. Business-to-business (or "B2B") is a recent darling of venture capitalists. Companies such as CheMatch and Fob, for example, provide electronic marketplaces for the chemical industry, allowing users to search for suppliers of raw materials and to negotiate prices on-line. Chemical manufacturers have formed a consortium called Elemica to provide a similar "e-hub"; founding members include industry heavyweights Dow, DuPont and BP Amoco.

One of the ironies of e-commerce to date [in 2001] is that Old Economy companies have reaped the real benefits. General Electric, for example, bought an estimated $6 billion worth of goods on the Web last year [2000], and each of its businesses sells products online. (The company's first Web page, for GE

Plastics, went up as early as October 1994.) Jack Welch, chairman and CEO, was recently quoted as saying, "The Internet was made for big companies."

Questions About Internet Business

Of course, this raises some of the same old questions about what business interests will do when left to their own devices. Business-to-business exchanges and consortia increase the possibility of anti-trust violations, as former rivals pool information about suppliers and perhaps fix prices. There's nothing new about corporate collusion, but compared with old-style negotiations, transactions online happen with lightning speed and cut across traditional boundaries. For that reason, the Federal Trade Commission is closely monitoring a proposed joint venture called Covisint, which involves big automakers like Ford, GM and Daimler-Chrysler.

More uncomfortable questions arise with e-commerce marketing—not the barrage of slick TV commercials and frenetic banner ads, but the bread-and-butter strategies that have yielded profits. These include the collection and distribution of customer information to other companies (or "data mining"), as well as direct email. Such strategies certainly exist in the real world, but Internet technologies make them faster and cheaper. A recent report from Forrester Research, a technology consulting firm, notes that while a paper catalog–mailing can cost a dollar a customer, junk email costs as little as five cents.

> *If Amazon is bought . . . all the information it has compiled about customers like you could be sold to the highest bidder.*

The low cost of direct, email isn't the only advantage that gets marketers' pulses racing. It's now possible for companies to track whether or not users open email solicitations, helping marketers to target their appeals to individual consumer interests. This is an outgrowth of technology that has allowed advertising companies like DoubleClick to follow where users travel on the Web and to identify which banner ads they click on. (Not many, apparently, since there's a reported one percent or less "clickthrough" rate for banners.) When somebody first visits a company's site, for example, an identifying code—or "cookie"—is placed on the user's computer. This allows the company to track where the user goes next, compiling information about whether she likes bird-watching, porno and/or designer luggage. Many online retailers such as Amazon.com also track individual buying patterns via cookies, which is how they know which options you've clicked before.

Loss of Privacy

Digital surfers may not like being tailed on the Web, but at least its constant stream of ads and bright graphics tip people off to the invasion. Cookies can be rejected through Web browsers like Netscape Navigator; alternatively, users can ask to be warned before accepting a cookie. In practice this is annoying, since the services many dotcoms provide are based on such "personalization." Still, it's another thing for marketers to weasel their way into personal email in-boxes. One Forrester survey predicts that by 2004, more than 200 billion email solicitations could be wafting our way.

HTML mail is the latest innovation, email software that can display graphics but also contains "Web bugs" notifying the sender when a message has been opened or forwarded. Superficially, Web bugs may seem like cookies, but an added twist has privacy advocates up in arms. While cookie codes are anonymous strings of numbers, HTML mail is linked to email addresses; these, in turn, can be matched with recipients' cookie codes, connecting far too many personal information dots. Not all users have software that can open HTML mail, but this past year [2001] the Federal Trade Commission was concerned enough to focus attention on the newest form of privacy invasion.

Many commercial Web sites now carry privacy notices, which are supposed to explain how customer information is used. But even if dotcoms claim they'd never sell user profiles based on cookies to unaffiliated third parties, what happens when that dotcom is bought by somebody else? For example, Amazon's Privacy Notice states: "Information about our customers is an important part of our business, and we are not in the business of selling it to others." Yet if readers slog to the end of this document, they'll also find the following disclaimer: "Our business changes constantly. This Notice and the Conditions of Use will change also, and use of information that we gather now is subject to the Privacy Notice in effect at the time of use." In other words, if Amazon is bought—a distinct possibility, given its rocky progress over the past year—all the information it has compiled about customers like you could be sold to the highest bidder.

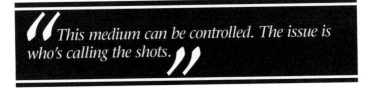

This medium can be controlled. The issue is who's calling the shots.

This doesn't have to be a horror story—How the New Economy Ate Our Hearts and Souls. Like so many complex endeavors that involve human beings, the rise of e-business is also an entertaining comedy of errors, and a reminder that people don't just lap up any absurdity offered them. Because the field is still new and the players keep jockeying, consumers can benefit from great deals and access to information. Sites like Travelocity.com can provide the cheapest air fares with just a few mouse clicks. Users can now read major newspapers for free online. And foes of Amazon.com take note: independent booksellers have formed a consortium with its own Web site: BookSense.com offers access to an array of independent bookstores around the country.

Marketing on the Internet

In the race to "build brand," consumer dotcoms are in more danger of ripping off themselves and investors than customers. But the farthest-reaching consequences of e-commerce will unfold in the marketing arena, because in this virtual space of words and images, stories can be endlessly spun and manipulated, making it harder than ever to identify corporate culprits. While Pets.com is no more, for example, the rights to the Sock Puppet character are up for sale as one of the defunct company's assets. In fact, this marketing tool was more popular than the company. In its heyday, hundreds of people sent fan email to the Puppet. Sales of Puppet dolls surpassed Pets.com's other products.

The Sock Puppet illustrates another form of co-optation. When he sang "Spinning Wheel" to a cat in a TV commercial, he reassured potential customers that they got the ironic joke and weren't corporate automatons. Just as companies like The Body Shop and Ben & Jerry's have appealed to baby-boomer consumers by seeming like anti-businesses, e-commerce continues to blur the boundaries between for-profit companies and everything else. In the dot-com universe, everyone is cool, everyone is hip and no one is fooled by politicians or stupid middle managers. It's an upscale, libertarian world in which business is a form of pop culture. It's a world where ultra-chic F——Company feeds on dot-com debacles at the same time that it runs banner ads and sells T-shirts.

But as legal scholar Lawrence Lessig points out in *Code and Other Laws of Cyberspace*, "The invisible hand, through commerce, is constructing an architecture that perfects control. . . ." Security protocols intended to protect information like credit-card numbers, for instance, are changing the nature of cyberspace. Despite the Silicon Valley belief that giving the market its head will assure both competitive and personal freedom, this medium can be controlled. The issue is who's calling the shots.

Consider the AOL/Time Warner merger. This will form a 41-billion-dollar media company, the largest in the world, with a combined, empire that spans broadcasting publishing, music and various kinds of Internet access. The Federal Trade Commission has been concerned about a number of anti-competitive consequences, and it approved the merger on the condition that the new entity be required to allow its rivals like Earthlink cable Internet access on Time Warner's extensive system. Yet a press release from the two companies still spun this restriction as a "commitment to consumer choice."

Here's the bug in the cyber-pretense of "consumer choice": the new medium may be revolutionary, but the forces that drive business are not. Pretty Web pages may not be enough to generate profits, but selling information about where customers go online does. As Lessig concludes in *Code*, "It is the age of the ostrich. We are excited about what we cannot know. We are proud to leave things to the invisible hand. We make the hand invisible by looking the other way." The trick, in this digital age of irony, is to look straight at what corporations do and to hold them accountable. Because it's the same old story despite the new spin: unregulated business activity, invasions of our private lives, and ads that claim everyone's a winner if they buy the Next Big Thing.

12

The Internet Is Instrumental in the Exploitation of Women and Children

Julie Pehar

Julie Pehar is co-owner of Equity Vision, an educational consulting firm in Toronto, Canada, dedicated to human rights education.

The Internet has become a breeding ground for the exploitation of women and children. This has occurred because of pervasive sexism and a lack of regulation. The mail-order bride industry, in particular, serves as an example of this exploitation because women are packaged and sold on the Internet as household labor or sexual playthings. These women can rarely speak their new country's language and are financially dependent upon their husbands. Mail-order bride sites also offer pornography and sex tourism services. Online services include live sex shows, computer-generated fantasies, and sexual settings in which the customer directs the performance—all now available to consumers in the privacy of their homes. This unprecedented growth of sex for sale on the Internet puts women and children at greater risk, and laws should be put into place to curb it. In addition, people need to be educated about both the Internet and the sexism that persists in society today.

Julie Pehar, "E-Brides: The Mail-Order Bride Industry and the Internet," *Canadian Woman Studies*, vol. 22, Spring 2003. Copyright © 2003 by *Canadian Woman Studies*. Reproduced by permission of the publisher and the author.

The Internet of today bears little resemblance to the primitive military inspired, free-net communications network of the 1950s and '60s. The involvement of corporations in the control of the Internet has encouraged a capitalistic undertone that has redirected the rather simple and questionably inclusive intentions of the early Internet. Instead, corporate ownership and control have manifested and glorified the acquisition of none other than a healthy bottom line. Quite simply, there are commodities for sale and privileged purchasers. This, in turn, has fueled a cyberworld which embodies favorable advances for some while simultaneously exposing the repugnant underbelly of racism, misogyny, classism, and heterosexism. Some researchers have asserted that the Internet has demonstrated an accelerated growth that mimics colonization of the past where western, English-speaking dominance has created extreme and often insurmountable power differentials between western and developing countries. Nevertheless, the Internet has become a ubiquitous reality.

Globally, issues of sexism and adherence to traditional gender normative behaviours have provided a basis for much discourse on the subordinate role women play in cyberspace. To further exacerbate inequality, the obscurity of cyberspace and its utopian image both serve to mask the transference of real world–inequality to cyber-inequality as the Internet merely reflects societal values, social structures and power hierarchies. Compounded by almost complete lack of regulation and enforceable legislation around safe and equitable usage, the Internet has become a breeding ground for exploitation.

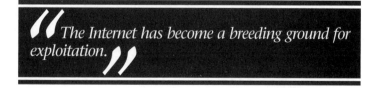

The Internet has become a breeding ground for exploitation.

In particular, the sexual exploitation of women and children has experienced an unprecedented explosion due to the enabling structure of the Internet. The Internet is now considered the preferred space for the buying and selling of women and children. Pre-existing widespread sexism, lack of formal regulation and increasing lack of control, but for only a few, have enabled sexual exploiters to become the commercial champions of the cyber world. Within a democratic and capitalistic framework, the championing of successful, though morally repugnant practice is rationalized and normalized. Though certainly not limited to the business of sex trafficking, many researchers have identified a conscious partnering between tech savvy entrepreneurs and vulnerable third world countries.

In this paper I will examine the "mail-order bride" industry and the sanctioning effects of the Internet and associated technologies in the exploitation of women and children. I will identify the inseparability between mail order brides, sex tourism, and pornography. I will challenge the notion that the Internet represents inevitable progress and democracy and I contend that the espoused knowledge, consensus and integrity the Internet claims to have, should and can be fiercely challenged.

The Mail-Order Bride Industry

The agents of the mail-order bride industry have moved from print magazines to the Internet as their preferred site of business. The Internet enables web pages to be updated regularly, inexpensively and with higher quality than print. The Internet reaches a wide global audience faster and more cheaply than any other medium. The on-line catalogues feature women, mostly from the Philippines, Asia and Eastern Europe shown with names, addresses, height, weight, education and hobbies. Some sites offer breast, hip and waist measurements and the ages of the women vary between 13 and 40 years old. The agents offer men assistance in finding a traditional wife who will put her husband and family before herself.

According to Marian Sciachitano [a professor in the Department of Women's Studies at Washington State University], "there are well over 10,000 links to sites on the World Wide Web (WWW) featuring mail-order brides or mail-order bride products and services." It is estimated that each year between 2,000 and 3,500 American men will find wives through the mail-order bride industry.

Currently, the vast majority of mail-order bride purchasers are heterosexual men from wealthy industrialized countries and the vast majority of the supply women are young, non-western, desperately poor women. Most grooms are seeking "youthful brides, often as young as thirteen."

Whether one considers such migration as exploitive or not there is a patriarchal and heteronormative undercurrent that presupposes the necessity for the industry at all. The gendered allocation of household labour including reproductive labour is a key element in the pervasive ideology of the mail-order bride industry.

Another important feature of the mail-order bride business is its relationship and inseparability from the sex tourism business. While proponents of bride trafficking claim that pornography and sex tourism are completely unrelated businesses, the marketing of complete services on the mail-order bride web sites tell a different story. Most companies that offer mail-order bride services also offer sex tours of third world countries. The Internet enables interconnectivity between the exploitation of minors internationally, positioning women and children both as potential brides and also as escorts while men tour third world countries buying sex whether the intention is to purchase a permanent woman or not.

Finally, there is little research on the social and cultural role for women who have migrated to a new country as a mail-order bride. It is widely recognized that migrant workers including mail-order brides are very vulnerable to physical, emotional, economic, and sexual abuse from their partners. Furthermore, migrant women often have language barriers that compound their disenfranchised and subordinate position. Children of western men and migrant wives may be visibly of mixed race and may experience exclusive and racist attitudes. Children are often used by men to maintain domestic compliance from their wives and the threat of deportation is constant. If migrant women are allowed or forced to work, they are often relegated to low paying, insecure, unskilled work with little government protection, and they often experience high degrees of sexism and racism. Most mail-order brides are completely financially dependent on their husbands and have little legal recourse in situations of abuse or unhappiness. The exploitive nature of migrant work is thus disguised in the illusion of the most palatable of cultural roles, that of wife and mother.

Further, many mail-order brides, in the context of women as migrant reproductive workers, are [as Yu Kojima[1] notes] "an instrument of economic activity and their remittances are regarded as a new form of capital accumulation." As Yu Kojima points out, migrant women who send money to family in their homelands "create substantial foreign exchange."

1. Yu Kojima is the author of *In the Business of Cultural Reproduction: Theoretical Implications of the Mail-Order Bride Phenomenon.*

The Role of the Internet

Concurrently, the Internet and all sex trade, tourism, trafficking and pornography are experiencing unprecedented growth. Donna Hughes [a professor in the Women's Studies Program at the University of Rhode Island] claims that "the Internet as a communications medium would exist without the sex industry, but the Internet industry would not be growing and expanding at its present rate without the sex industry." In 1998, it was estimated that 69 percent of the total Internet content sales were related to adult content. Jonathon Coopersmith [an associate professor of history at Texas A&M University] reminds us that what is driving the transformation of the sex industry technology has been "the great capitalist engines of innovation and the quest for profits." Internet pornography has become the highest growth, highest profit market ever known.

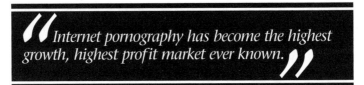

Internet pornography has become the highest growth, highest profit market ever known.

Pornography previously in print form quickly adapted to the immeasurable advantages of going on-line. From 1994 to 1997, *Playboy* and other mainstream publications moved to the web and met with unprecedented growth. The Internet however, did a lot more than simply boost pornography sales. According to Coopersmith, "the environment and nature of a pornographic experience has altered." The previously passive experience of print images has been replaced by live person-to-person videos and audio transmissions. Suddenly, live sex shows, virtual fantasies, and consumer-directed sexual scenarios are right in our homes and offices at the touch of a mouse. Consumers can choose a woman or child from anywhere in the world and demand and view live sexual acts. As Donna Hughes concludes, "the electronic merger of pornography and prostitution has arrived." The Internet has decreased the cost of accessing pornography while increasing the interactivity, speed, ease and privacy for users.

Within this framework, the global properties of the World Wide Web have created a market where there is an insatiable demand for the commodity of sexualized women and children. Moreover, children worldwide are now at greater risk than ever before as the Internet facilitates a communications medium which allows sexual predators to network, encourage and support each other. As Madeleine Plasencia [a professor at the University of Tulsa College of Law] explains:

> The Internet has provided the horizontal parallax over which all can participate in communication and transaction, education and entertainment. The rise of this advanced technology has led to a new red light district where children worldwide are now at greater risk.

Defunct of moral accountability, the business practices of the sex industry are tough to match. The industry has mastered privacy, security and fast payment transactions as well as data base management expertise.

A Struggle for Power

Ellen Rose [an associate professor in education at the University of New Brunswick in Canada] asserts that a marginalized "Other" is created that does not necessarily involve a physical exertion of power but a hegemonic power enforced by a few at the expense of many. She continues, "what we see today is a different kind of power struggle and conquest: a global renegotiation of margins and centres, in which authority is imposed on the basis of demonstrated technological superiority."

Popular discourse on information technology often refers to the creation of a digital divide or in other words, information haves and have-nots. Ellen Rose concludes, "on a wired planet, the third world suddenly becomes not a place but a condition, an Othering based on an inability to maintain technological currency."

Issues of racism and sexism permeate the cyberworld. [Activist and writer] Susan Hawthorne agrees when she states that:

> whiteness is not visible to the powerful, because they themselves are white. They notice bodies that are not white and they impute a difference of those imaginations. They notice them as cultural. But whiteness to the white, is the norm. It has a normative status in the same way that man has a normative status.

The concept of difference feeds the sexual curiosity of

some. Sciachitano relates the concept of difference to people living in first world countries who feel familiar with the role (though paternalistic) of missionaries civilizing and rescuing primitive "others." Actually, this reinforces the

> Orientalist male-power-fantasy and considering the subjective locations of Asian and Pacific mail-order brides, their female bodies are being positioned as exotic products to be trafficked via these newly established electronic commerce trade routes.

As bell hooks [a professor of English at City College in New York] contends:

> The mail-order bride web sites are now the contemporary virtual vehicles for re-enacting and re-ritualizing this U.S. imperialistic fantasy of power and desire for seduction via a neocolonial cyberspace journey. White males claim the body of the colored Other instrumentally, as unexplored terrain, a symbolic frontier that will be fertile ground for their reconstruction of the white, western, heterosexual masculine norm.

Women and Choice

It is clear that around the world women and children remain increasingly vulnerable to sexual exploitation in light of an exploding Internet sex industry. Compounding their vulnerability as women and children, refugee and migrant women are at increased risk especially considering most are suffering from devastating poverty, racism, and economically impoverished home lives. However, many sex-industry owners claim that women choose to participate in the sex trade work or bride trafficking as a means to make money or improve their social status. They further claim that women gain empowerment from making their own decisions. I do not impose judgment on anyone's decisions whether I feel they are made without fair knowledge and advantage or not. However, according to Hughes,

> the men buying women and posting the information see and perceive the events from their self-interested perspective. Their awareness of racism, colonization, global economic inequalities and, of course, sexism, is limited to how these forces ben-

efit them. A country's economic or political crisis and the accompanying poverty are advantages, which produce cheap women for the men.

Moreover, as Sciachitano states, "while it may appear to be a better alternative to the options available at home, from both first and third world perspectives, it is mired in U.S./Western cultural mythologies and imperialistic nostalgia."

> **//** *Unbridled commitment toward effective and safe laws for women and children around the world must be a priority.* **//**

What is problematic for me as a white woman living in Canada is attempting to impose an ethnocentric perspective on women coping with circumstances that are completely foreign to me. I am not neutral and I acknowledge my limitations. What seems most useful to me is to respect and value the resilience, honour, and strength of all women who, for whatever reason, choose to work in the sex trade or bride trafficking industries and get down to the difficult business of making meaningful long-term change. I believe that all women need helpful, protective strategies to ensure dignity and safety in their lives until large-scale change begins. Structural change is imperative. We also need to hear from women. There is little research that includes personal accounts or sharing of perspectives from women who have lived this experience.

Combating Exploitation

It is time to look at how the Internet has developed and the conditions that have made access to the Interact so easy for some and so difficult for others. We need to ensure that both men and women, boys and girls have educational initiatives in their schools to ensure equal understanding of the technology as an analytical forum, not simply a tool of communication. Inequities of language, control, access, and usage need to be common knowledge so that the advancement of technology will be met with scrutiny and caution. I believe that much accountability lies with those who control and manage the Internet. Certainly universal misogyny and racism are central to the sexualization of women and this, in turn, supports sexual exploitation. These changes will be slow and must be attacked from many directions. In the meantime, recognition of the partnership between technology, exploitation, and the enabling features of globalization should be paramount.

Vigilant evaluation and challenge to the patriarchal structures that maintain prescriptive ideologies around reproductive and family roles must continue. We need to encourage a reversal of the gaze, the stare, the curiosity about the "othered" women and issue a challenge to ourselves, our political policies, our educational policies, our family structures, our entertainment, and our use of technology in the exploitation of women.

Identifying prostitution, pornography, sex tourism, and bride trafficking as connected through the commonality of violence against women is a crucial factor. Without the acknowledgement from societal institutions that they are linked, women's agency will be compromised. Every level of government and all societal institutional pillars must understand the selling of women's and children's bodies as an affront to their human rights. Unbridled commitment toward effective and safe laws for women and children around the world must be a priority.

We can stop advertising the selling of women and children if we choose. We can attempt to legislate and criminalize the smuggling of women and children from country to country. We can destroy or make difficult the cyber communities of men who fuel and spread misogynist information about women as dispensable sexual objects. We can stop protecting the identity of sex trade users. We must continue to fight at every level so as to protect all children from sexual predators. We must protect women when they come here to live. We need to understand what makes a woman vulnerable when she is here, her language barriers, cultural differences, financial dependence, and offer access to support and friendships. Lastly, we must have compassion and respect for the millions of women who find themselves in positions as sex workers or trafficked brides. They deserve our continued commitment for seeking understanding and effective and practical laws to keep them, and their children, safe.

13

The Internet Can Be Dangerous for Children

Janet Stanley

Janet Stanley is a researcher with the National Child Protection Clearinghouse at the Australian Institute of Family Studies. She is the coauthor of In the Firing Line: Violence and Power in Child Protection Work.

The Internet poses a serious danger for children because it is uncensored and unregulated. For example, children are regularly exposed to violent and sexual material, which can be extremely distressing for them. In addition, sexual offenders prey upon children in chat rooms, often persuading the children to engage in sexual activity with them. Children are used in pornographic Web sites as well, normalizing pedophilia and making it easier to objectify children. The government and other organizations need to work to curb Internet child abuse.

It is said that children in the United States spend more time with electronic media than they spend in any other activity, except sleep. There is a long history of research on the impact on children of watching violence on television and film, which reveals an association between exposure to dramatic violence and violent behaviour in children. In contrast, there has been very little research on the impact of the internet on children. This is despite the fact that as the availability and use of the internet expands, increasing numbers of children are being exposed to content via the internet, which has already been judged to be inappropriate for children in other media outlets, such as television and film. In addition, through their use of the internet, children are being involved in activities considered to be abusive in other contexts, such as sexual exploitation. . . .

While there have been some moves to protect children from aspects of the internet, the issue of child exploitation through the internet has not entered the mainstream discourse in the field of child abuse and neglect. Rather, child protection in relation to this medium is seen as a matter which largely needs to be addressed by parents and children themselves, guided by advice from the government and other organisations. . . .

Children's Internet Access

The internet is a medium that facilitates access and communication between people, which is direct and private. While this new medium has considerable benefits, the downside is that, unlike most other information and communication sources available to children, the internet is largely uncensored and only partially regulated. Children live mainly in an environment where most information is filtered by parents, carers and teachers, where television and film content is regulated to some extent, and where a person has to be 18 years of age or over to access "adult" content and venues.

Despite the development of some measures aimed at preventing children's access to inappropriate material on the internet, such as filtering software and the production of guidelines for internet use, these processes have not been particularly effective. Children are still accessing unsuitable and highly offensive sites and are being exploited and abused on the internet, both directly and indirectly.

Exposure to Inappropriate Material

Children may be exposed to inappropriate material on the internet, such as sexual and violent material and pornography featuring both adults and children. It would seem that the internet has promoted the pornography industry as it probably provides the largest collection of pornography currently available, including sexual chat channels, pictures and text. A recent press release from the Australian Minister for Justice and Customs reports that about 85 per cent of child pornography seized in Australia is distributed via the internet.

Australian research, which sampled 200 children, found that 38 per cent of boys and two per cent of girls aged 16 and 17 years deliberately use the internet to see sexually explicit material. They also found that 84 per cent of surveyed boys and 60 per cent of girls had unwanted exposure to sexual material. As the authors note, the discrepancy between desired and undesired exposure, particularly for girls (two per cent desired and 60 per cent undesired), is of considerable concern, as it would appear that exposure is difficult to avoid.

A study from the United States on children aged between 10 and 17 years placed the level of undesired exposure much lower than this, at 25 per cent. However, this figure could at least partially be explained by the inclusion of younger children in the American study, who are less likely to undertake independent exploring on the internet. Of additional concern is the fact that many children (for example, 43 per cent of those in the United States study) do not report this exposure.

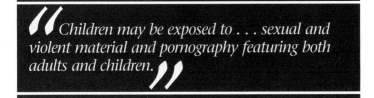

Children may be exposed to . . . sexual and violent material and pornography featuring both adults and children.

The Australian research which explored the exposure of teenage children to both X-rated videos and sex sites on the internet, found the internet pornographic content involved much more violent, extreme, and deviant behaviour than was found in videos. In addition, the internet presented sex as "divorced from intimacy, loving affection, and human connection", it commodified, subjugated and degraded the role of women and showed non-consensual sexual assaults. . . .

No research has been undertaken on the longer-term impact of exposure to pornography on children under 14 years. . . . The long-term impact of this exposure—whether it causes "psychological, moral, or developmental harm to children"—is not known. Research that has been undertaken on pornography use has been entirely on desired and anticipated exposure. However, Australian research concludes that, in relation to one aspect of this problem, evidence of the association between adult use of certain pornography and sexual aggression provides grounds for "serious concern" where children are exposed to this material.

The small amount of research on the shorter-term response of children to offensive material suggests that some children are being severely affected. About a quarter of the children in the American study (24 per cent) reported being "very or extremely upset by the exposure", with younger children experiencing the most distress.

The Sexual Exploitation of Children

Interactive communication on the internet, such as chat rooms, offer child sexual offenders additional means of accessing children. This technology provides a means by which children can be groomed or prepared for sexual use, in a context where the child is usually alone and therefore susceptible to influence and persuasion by the offender. An offender uses misinformation and deception, often misrepresenting him/herself as a child or a friend. Offenders may include threats and techniques such as blaming the child for the illicit interaction, or the use of behaviour suggestive of positive interaction (such as attentive and apparently caring behaviour), thus making it difficult for even parents to identify inappropriateness. The internet allows potential offenders into a child's environment which is usually perceived as being safe—home, schools, libraries and friends' houses—thus providing mixed messages and ambiguity about reality for children.

The aim of the offender may be to engage in cyber-sex or virtual sexual activity with the child, and/or persuade the child to meet with the offender. Research from the United States has found that 19 per cent of 10–17 year olds who regularly use the internet have experienced an unwanted sexual solicitation or approach in the previous year. Research from Scotland has shown that 49 per cent of children who use the web have taken part in a sexually explicit conversation with another person in a chat room. Based on the figures from the United States study, it is possible that over 50,000 Australian children are approached annually for sexual purposes.

The Use of Children in Child Pornography

The internet provides an additional medium to existing venues for the distribution of child pornography. It is difficult to make definitive statements about whether the child pornography industry is growing. However, it is certainly more visible and the nature of the internet, which provides ease of access and storage, secrecy and anonymity, suggests that there is likely to be an increase in use of pornography.

It would appear that some offenders collect child pornography pictures, and often text, for their private use only. Time is spent sorting and classifying the pictures, sometimes to the point where the behaviour becomes addictive. However, others use child pornography to facilitate the seduction of new victims, for sexual arousal and to feed sexual fantasies. Commercial opportunists have entered the market for child pornography and charge for the provision of material and access to pornographic sites. An item on *BBC News* [in 2003] reported the recent arrest of a man who had sold over 250,000 downloads to people in 60 countries, which to date has resulted in 1,600 arrests in Great Britain.

> *49 per cent of children who use the web have taken part in a sexually explicit conversation with another person in a chat room.*

Whatever the end use, the production of child pornography usually requires a child to be sexually abused, either through actual events or the use of morphing or digitally altering photographs. There has been little research on who the children used for pornography are. One unpublished study found the children were more likely to be from homes with high discord, often where there was child and drug abuse. It has also been found that children who have experienced neglect are more likely to be used in the production of child pornography.

The Internet Normalises Pedophilia

The internet features of accessibility, privacy and low cost serve to encourage some offences. For example, child pornography is often used by offenders to groom children by "normalising" sexual activity with children and breaking down inhibitions, or to blackmail a child into desired behaviour by threatening to expose their use of pornography. Indeed, the saturation of the internet with such material may serve to "normalise" this behaviour and probably makes it easier to objectify children as sexual artefacts. Pornography is also thought to reinforce a person's sexual attraction to children.

While the small amount of research that is available as yet provides no clear answers, there are suggestions that an increase in exposure to child pornography stimulates some people to move from viewing child pornography to engaging in the sexual exploitation of children. In a study of 150 paedophiles, slightly more than one in three reported using child pornographic materials shortly before committing a sexual offence.

There are some suggestions that the internet may encourage people who were previously not offenders to engage in sexual offending. While the child sexual offender is almost always profiled as a mature-aged male, findings from research in the United States report that child sexual offenders who use the internet appear to have a different profile. In this study nearly half of the offenders were under 18 years of age with few over 25 years, about one-third being female. While this needs to be verified with further research, it has been reported that Australian adolescents are becoming increasingly involved in e-crime in general. . . .

Websites and Virtual Communities

The internet provides information, and often opinions, on a vast array of topics, including the promotion of activities which may be viewed as abusive of children. For example, while many websites are opposed to the physical punishment of children, it is possible to find others which argue for the use of physical punishment, many of which present information in the context of academic or religious authority.

Other sites are maintained by proponents for sexual relations with children, such as the group NAMBLA, the North American Man/Boy Love Association. The content of this site "justifies, rationalises and normalises" members' behaviours through newsletters, brochures and booklets, claiming the child will be a willing and active participant in a sexual event.

The establishment of virtual communities, or a fairly stable network of like-minded people, offers a supportive environment to pursue and promote a particular interest. Internet child pornography communities have been established where child pornography is both validated and justified. Status in this community is achieved through the extent of a person's collection of pornographic material and the ability to contribute new material. Such groups provide empowerment to the paedophile, a person often marginalised in society, while at the same time allowing him to remain anonymous. . . .

The internet allows child sexual offenders to function more easily as it provides an environment where conventional means of access to children, and the need for social skills, are broken down. . . .

Recognising and Responding to Internet Abuse

One of "the major lessons of history is that adults prefer not to see most child abuse", or find it too difficult to believe. There is a risk that history is repeating itself in relation to child exploitation and the internet. Greater recognition of how the internet can be used as a weapon to abuse and exploit children will hopefully lead to the provision of prevention and intervention measures. Some measures are being taken. For example, the Australian Government recently announced an increase in jail terms of up to ten years for the possession and distribution of internet child pornography.

However, it would appear that, in general, measures to protect children from abuse through the internet are proving to be less than adequate. Regulation of pornography on the internet is reported to be "manifestly failing". The internet filtering software, NetNanny, recommended by all three of Australia's largest internet providers, has been found to be ineffective, failing to block sites 38 per cent of the time. . . . Home use of the software is as low as one per cent of their customers.

Much of the prevention response presently in place relies on parental supervision. However, these measures have been found to be of "marginal utility" in a major study from the United States [by K.J. Mitchell, D. Finkelhor and J. Wolak, 2003]. Responsibility for protection has been given to parents rather than to the broader community, and indeed, the internet industry itself. . . .

While there is a need for more research about how the internet impacts on children, enough is already known to begin to take action to protect children. Recommendations for policies and actions that could give children greater protection while they use the internet, include the need for a move from self-regulation by Internet Service Providers to more stringent government regulation and review of the law enforcement process.

Organizations to Contact

The editors have compiled the following list of organizations concerned with the issues debated in this book. The descriptions are derived from materials provided by the organizations. All have publications or information available for interested readers. The list was compiled on the date of publication of the present volume; names, addresses, phone and fax numbers, and e-mail addresses may change. Be aware that many organizations take several weeks or longer to respond to inquiries, so allow as much time as possible.

American Library Association (ALA)
50 E. Huron, Chicago, IL 60611
(800) 545-2433
Web site: www.ala.org

The ALA is a trade organization representing America's librarians that provides leadership for the development, promotion, and improvement of library and information services and the profession of librarianship. The ALA supports free access to library materials and resources and opposes the Children's Internet Protection Act, which went into effect on July 1, 2004, and requires public libraries to install content-filtering software on computers with Internet access. The ALA publishes the magazine *American Libraries* and the *Newsletter on Intellectual Freedom*.

Berkman Center for Internet and Society
Harvard Law School
Baker House, 1587 Massachusetts Ave., Cambridge, MA 02138
(617) 495-7547 • fax: (617) 495-7641
e-mail: cyber@law.harvard.edu
Web site: http://cyber.law.harvard.edu

The Berkman Center is a research program that was founded to explore cyberspace, share in its study, and help pioneer its development. Intellectual property issues on the Internet are among the program's main topics of interest. The program's Web site offers a wealth of papers and news stories on Internet piracy, copyright, and Internet regulation issues.

Bridges.org
1424 Sixteenth St. NW, Suite 502, Washington, DC 20036
(202) 299-0120 • fax: (202) 318-7792
e-mail: info@bridges.org • Web site: www.bridges.org

Bridges.org is an international nonprofit organization that works to help span the digital divide. Bridges.org researches, tests, and promotes the best practices for sustainable, empowering use of information and communication technology. The organization publishes reports, research, and position papers.

Cato Institute
1000 Massachusetts Ave. NW, Washington, DC 20001
(202) 842-0200 • fax: (202) 842-3490
Web site: www.cato.org

The Cato Institute is a libertarian public policy research foundation. It opposes government regulation of the Internet, including government efforts to tax the Internet and to restrict Internet gambling and e-mail spam. Cato publishes the magazine *Regulation* and its Web site includes several reports on Internet issues, such as *The Digital Dirty Dozen: The Most Destructive High-Tech Legislative Measures of the 107th Congress* and *Internet Privacy and Self-Regulation: Lessons from the Porn Wars*, along with many shorter opinion pieces.

Center for Democracy and Technology (CDT)
1634 I St. NW, Suite 1100, Washington, DC 20006
(202) 637-9800 • fax: (202) 637-0968
e-mail: feedback@cdt.org • Web site: www.cdt.org

CDT's mission is to develop public policy solutions that advance constitutional civil liberties and democratic values in the new computer and communications media. Pursuing its mission through policy research, public education, and coalition building, the center works to increase citizens' privacy and the public's control over the use of personal information held by government and other institutions. Its publications include the reports *Considering Consumer Privacy, Broadband Access: Maximizing the Democratic Potential of the Internet,* and *Why Am I Getting All This Spam?,* as well as issue briefs and policy papers.

Computer Professionals for Social Responsibility (CPSR)
PO Box 717, Palo Alto, CA 94302
(650) 322-3778 • fax: (650) 322-4748
e-mail: cpsr@cpsr.org • Web site: www.cpsr.org

CPSR provides the public and policy makers with realistic assessments of the power, promise, and problems of information technology. CPSR members work to direct public attention to critical choices concerning the applications of information technology and how those choices affect society. It publishes the quarterly *CPSR Journal* and the *PING!* newsletter.

Digital Promise Project
1717 K St. NW, Suite 209, Washington, DC 20036
(202) 454-4683 • fax: (202) 675-1010
e-mail: info@digitalpromise.org • Web site: www.digitalpromise.org

Digital Promise's goal is to unlock the potential of the Internet and other new information technologies for education. It funds efforts to train teachers in the use of information technology and to digitize educational resources. The report *Creating the Digital Opportunity Investment Trust (DO IT): A Proposal to Transform Learning and Training for the 21st Century* is available for download on the organization's Web site.

Electronic Frontier Foundation (EFF)
454 Shotwell St., San Francisco, CA 94110-1914
(415) 436-9333 • fax: (415) 436-9993
e-mail: information@eff.org • Web site: www.eff.org

EFF is an organization of students and other individuals that aims to promote a better understanding of telecommunications issues. It fosters awareness of civil liberties issues arising from advancements in computer-based communications media and supports litigation to preserve, protect, and extend First Amendment rights in computing and Internet technologies. EFF publishes a comprehensive archive of digital civil liberties information on its Web site.

Electronic Privacy Information Center (EPIC)
1718 Connecticut Ave. NW, Suite 200, Washington, DC 20009
(202) 483-1140 • fax: (202) 483-1248
Web site: www.epic.org

EPIC is a public interest research center that works to focus public attention on emerging civil liberties issues and to protect privacy, the First Amendment, and constitutional values. It supports privacy-protection legislation and provides information on how individuals can protect their online privacy. EPIC publishes the *EPIC Alert* newsletter and the *Privacy Law Sourcebook*.

Free Expression Policy Project (FEPP)
Brennan Center for Justice at NYU School of Law
Democracy Program, Free Expression Policy Project
161 Avenue of the Americas, 12th Fl., New York, NY 10013
(212) 992-8847 • fax: (212) 995-4550
Web site: www.fepproject.org

The project provides research and analysis on difficult censorship issues and seeks free speech–friendly solutions to the concerns that drive censorship campaigns. It opposes the restriction of information and free speech on the Internet that could result from copyright and antipornography legislation. FEPP policy reports include *Internet Filters* and *The Progress of Science and Useful Arts*, which deals with Internet copyright.

Internet Society (ISOC)
1775 Wiehle Ave., Suite 102, Reston, VA 20190
(703) 326-9880 • fax: (703) 326-9881
e-mail: isoc@isoc.org • Web site: www.isoc.org

ISOC is a professional membership society that addresses issues confronting the future of the Internet and is the organization home for the groups responsible for Internet infrastructure standards. ISOC acts as a global clearinghouse for Internet information and education and coordinates Internet-related initiatives. The society organizes conferences, provides training workshops, performs market research, and publishes information on its Web site and in its *ISOC Member Briefings*. It also publishes *"E" on the Internet* magazine and the *Internet Report* catalog, which documents the technology, protocols, and procedures that form the Internet.

Morality in Media
475 Riverside Dr., Suite 239, New York, NY 10115
(212) 870-3222 • fax: (212) 870-2765
e-mail: mim@moralityinmedia.org
Web site: www.moralityinmedia.org

Morality in Media is a national not-for-profit organization established in 1962 to combat obscenity and uphold decency standards in the media. It maintains the National Obscenity Law Center, a clearinghouse of legal materials on obscenity law, and conducts public information programs to educate and involve concerned citizens. It supports efforts to restrict pornography on the Internet, including pornographic spam. The Morality in Media Web site offers several articles and issue overviews.

Pew Internet and American Life Project
1100 Connecticut Ave. NW, Suite 710, Washington, DC 20036
(202) 296-0019 • fax: (202) 296-6797
e-mail: webmaster@pewinternet.org • Web site: www.pewinternet.org

The nonprofit Pew Internet and American Life Project collects data about Internet use and produces reports that explore the impact of the Internet on families, communities, work and home, daily life, education, health care, and civic and political life. Its many reports include *The Internet as a Unique News Source, Faith Online, Older Americans and the Internet,* and *Spam: How It Is Hurting Email and Degrading Life on the Internet.*

P2P United
Adam Eisgrau, Executive Director, c/o Flanagan Consulting LLC
1317 F St. NW, Suite 800, Washington, DC 20004
Web site: www.p2punited.org

P2P United is the unified voice of the peer-to-peer technology industry's leading companies and proponents. P2P United represents and champions the P2P industry and technology to policy makers, opinion leaders, the media, and the public. The organization does not support Internet piracy and disputes the idea that Internet file sharing is mainly a tool for illegal copying. The organization's Web site offers issue overviews and news updates on legal and technological developments in the P2P field.

U.S. Internet Industry Association (USIIA)
815 Connecticut Ave. NW, Suite 620, Washington, DC 20006
(703) 924-0006 • fax: (703) 924-4203
Web site: www.usiia.org

Established in 1994, USIIA is a nonprofit trade association for Internet commerce, content, and connectivity. The association advocates effective public policy for the Internet and provides business news as well as information on upcoming legislation, spam and viruses, and industry conferences. USIIA publishes a weekly newsletter, the *USIIA Bulletin.*

World Future Society (WFS)
7910 Woodmont Ave., Suite 450, Bethesda, MD 20814
(800) 989-8274 • fax: (301) 951-0394
e-mail: info@wfs.org • Web site: www.wfs.org

The WFS is an association of people interested in how social and technological developments are shaping the future. It serves as a clearinghouse for ideas about the future. The society publishes the *Futurist,* a bimonthly magazine, and hosts the Cyber Society Forum on its Web site, where participants submit essays on the future of information technology.

Bibliography

Books

R. Michael Alvarez
and Thad E. Hall

Point, Click, and Vote: The Future of Internet Voting. Washington, DC: Brookings Institution, 2004.

David M. Anderson
and Michael
Cornfield, eds.

The Civic Web: Online Politics and Democratic Values. Lanham, MD: Rowman & Littlefield, 2003.

Aaron Ben-Ze'ev

Love Online: Emotions on the Internet. New York: Cambridge University Press, 2004.

Edward Burman

Shift! The Unfolding Internet: Hype, Hope, and History. Hoboken, NJ: Wiley, 2003.

Michael Cornfield

Politics Moves Online: Campaigning and the Internet. New York: Century Foundation, 2004.

David Crystal

Language and the Internet. New York: Cambridge University Press, 2001.

Pamela Donovan

No Way of Knowing: Crime, Urban Legends, and the Internet. New York: Routledge, 2004.

Greg Elmer, ed.

Critical Perspectives on the Internet. Lanham, MD: Rowman & Littlefield, 2002.

David Gauntlett and
Ross Horsley, eds.

Web Studies. New York: Oxford University Press, 2004.

Rachel Gibson,
Paul Nixon, and
Stephen Ward, eds.

Political Parties and the Internet: Net Gain? New York: Routledge, 2003.

Preston Gralla

How the Internet Works. Indianapolis: Pearson Education, 2003.

Sarah L. Holloway
and Gill Valentine

Cyberkids: Children in the Information Age. New York: Routledge Falmer, 2003.

Philip N. Howard
and Steve Jones, eds.

Society Online: The Internet in Context. Thousand Oaks, CA: Sage, 2004.

Dennis W. Johnson

Congress Online: Bridging the Gap Between Citizens and Their Representatives. New York: Routledge, 2004.

Tim Jordan and
Paul A. Taylor

Hacktivism and Cyberwars: Rebels with a Cause? New York: Routledge, 2004.

Jonathan Land

The Spam Letters. San Francisco: No Starch, 2004.

Martha McCaughey
and Michael D.
Ayers, eds.

Cyberactivism: Online Activism in Theory and Practice. New York: Routledge, 2003.

Roger W. Morrell, ed. *Older Adults, Health Information, and the World Wide Web.* Mahwah, NJ: Lawrence Erlbaum, 2002.

Nathan Newman *Net Loss: Internet Prophets, Private Profits, and the Costs to Community.* University Park: Pennsylvania State University Press, 2002.

Andrea Orr *Meeting, Mating, and Cheating: Sex, Love, and the New World of Online Dating.* Upper Saddle River, NJ: Reuters, 2004.

Jenny Pickerill *Cyberprotest: Environmental Activism Online.* New York: Manchester University Press, 2003.

Sally Richards *Futurenet: The Past, Present, and Future of the Internet as Told by Its Creators and Visionaries.* New York: Wiley, 2002.

Leslie Regan Shade *Gender and Community in the Social Construction of the Internet.* New York: Peter Lang, 2002.

Max Taylor and Ethel Quayle *Child Pornography: An Internet Crime.* New York: Brunner-Routledge, 2003.

Adam Thierer and Clyde Wayne Crews Jr. *Who Rules the Net? Internet Governance and Jurisdiction.* Washington, DC: Cato Institute, 2003.

Anton Vedder *Ethics and the Internet.* Antwerp, Belgium: Intersentia, 2001.

Patricia Wallace *The Internet in the Workplace: How New Technology Is Transforming Work.* New York: Cambridge University Press, 2004.

Jason Whittaker *The Cyberspace Handbook.* New York: Routledge, 2004.

Periodicals

Zoe Arthur and Baird Lupia "Can Web Sites Change Citizens? Implications of Web White and Blue," *PS: Political Science & Politics,* January 2003.

Randy Barrett "Safety Net: In the Wake of Terrorist Attacks, the Net Provides Data, Communication, Links to Relief Effort," *Interactive Week,* September 17, 2001.

Alan Bass "Shifting the Balance: Citizens, Employers, Journalists, and the Internet," *Textual Studies in Canada,* Fall 2002.

David Batstone "Click Here for Cupid," *Sojourners,* April 2004.

Manuel Castells "The Cultures of the Internet," *Queen's Quarterly,* Fall 2002.

Elaine M. Cummings "Women in the Developing World," *CIO,* Fall/Winter 2003.

John C. Dvorak "Lies! Lies! and Suckers," *PC Magazine,* February 23, 2004.

Economist "Only Disconnect," January 25, 2003.

Susannah Fox and Lee Rainie   "E-Patients and the Online Health Care Revolution," *Physician Executive*, November/December 2002.

Jane Gershaw   "The Internet as Antidepressant," *Inside MS*, Spring 2001.

Reid Goldsborough   "New Media and Disasters," *Black Issues in Higher Education*, November 8, 2001.

Todd Hanson   "Our World Is Changing, Faster Now than Ever," *Healthcare Review*, August 5, 2003.

Philip Jenkins   "Bringing the Loathsome to Light," *Chronicle of Higher Education*, March 1, 2002.

Shirley Duglin Kennedy   "Looks Like It's Time for the Internet: If There's Something You Want to Know, You Can Find It Instantly on the Web," *Information Today*, June 2002.

Olga Kharif   "The Net: Now, Folks Can't Live Without It," *Business Week Online*, June 10, 2003.

Charles L. Klotzer   "The Revolution We Were Waiting for Has Arrived—Virtually," *St. Louis Journalism Review*, September 2003.

Yuval Levin   "Politics After the Internet," *Public Interest*, Fall 2002.

Eric Metcalf   "A Web of Addictions: Internet Obsessions Could Hurt Your Loved Ones Financially, Emotionally, and Physically," *Better Homes and Gardens*, May 2003.

Timothy J. Mullaney   "The E-Biz Surprise: It Wasn't All Hype. For Companies as Well as Consumers, E-Commerce Is Hotter than Ever," *Business Week*, May 12, 2003.

John Patrick   "The Ultimate Internet," *Network World*, November 10, 2003.

David Piscitello and Stephen Kent   "The Sad and Increasingly Deplorable State of Internet Security," *Business Communications Review*, February 2003.

Janet Rae-Dupree   "Piecing Together the Internet," *U.S. News & World Report*, April 22, 2002.

Rene Ryman   "The Internet as a Forum for Political Participation," *Computer & Internet Lawyer*, January 2004.

Timothy L. Thomas   "Al Qaeda and the Internet: The Danger of 'Cyberplanning,'" *Parameters*, Spring 2003.

Tom R. Tyler   "Is the Internet Changing Social Life? It Seems the More Things Change, the More They Stay the Same," *Journal of Social Issues*, Spring 2002.

Daniel Tynan   "Spam Inc.," *PC World*, August 2002.

Index

112